PUPUS TO DA MAX

Written and Researched by
PAT SASAKI
DOUGLAS SIMONSON
KEN SAKATA

Cartoon Ideas Sweated Out by
DOUGLAS SIMONSON
PAT SASAKI
KEN SAKATA
TREMAINE TAMAYOSE

Cartoons Drawn, Re-drawn, and
Re-drawn Again by
DOUGLAS SIMONSON (PEPPO)

Published by
BESS PRESS
P.O. Box 22388
Honolulu, Hawaii 96822

Bess Press, Inc.
P.O. Box 22388
Honolulu, HI 96822

**This book is dedicated to everybody in
Hawaii who likes to grind.**

ACKNOWLEDGMENTS

Special thanks to ANN CORUM and RANDY CHUN, who both took the time to go through the manuscript of this book and make corrections and suggestions.

Aaron Paragoso, Garrick Higuchi, Lillian & Herman Sakata, Dorothy Hoe, We Care, Barbara & Tom Takata, Randy and Michelle Sasaki, Profitability Consulting, Aaron Fujioka, Glenna Sakata, Cathy Camilo, Tremaine Tamayose, Ronald Wong, Gail Haruki, Jenny Kaleikini, Stuart W. Lesses, Tad & Ardie James, June Takenaka, Light, Inc., Stuart Novick, Barbara Tong, Chester Akamine, Aileen Shin, Holly Williams, Warren Banao, Nan Asuncion, Thomas Casillano, Charles Roylo, Steve Miller, Chinatown Merchants, Rep. Marshall Ige, Kevin Iwamoto, Victoria Lam, Dennis Fujitake, Wilbert Ching, Reiko Ibano, Joyce Fujimoto, Brad Lum, Anju Suzuki, Susan Dela Cruz, Romeo Callado, Stuart Ching, Pris Fujioka, Ahn Family, Ellen Katoda, Laurie Levine, Dana Hall, Linda G. McEvoy, Ladies at Hale No Na Wahine, Stanton Ching, Charles Roylo, Gerri Kaneshiro, Ritsuko Nishida, Kathy Liu, Brett Uprichard, Plaza Manila.

Typesetting by
STATS 'N GRAPHICS

INTRODUCTION

The book you are holding in your hands is unlike any other book ever created in Hawaii. It's the first-ever dictionary of local foods. No one has ever attempted something like this before. And now that we've done it, we know why.

We know we haven't even begun to do justice to all the cultures that have brought their cuisines with them to Hawaii. This book would be about eight times as long if we had kept going. We tried to hit the high points and define the most popular, best-known ethnic dishes and ingredients, and if we left out your favorite, we're sorry. But feel free to use the back page and write to us and let us know what we left out!

Now just because we have a reputation for writing funny stuff, don't think this is all made up. THIS IS FO' REAL, BRAH. We did a lot of research. The recipes are for real too! Try 'em! We had 'em tested by some of our good friends whose kokua we really appreciate.

We hope you enjoy this book. If you like to eat . . . and you like to laugh . . . we know you will!

Aloha,

Ken
Pat
Peppo

BIBLIOGRAPHY

Claudio, Virginia Serraon. **Dictionary of Foods.** Manila: G.M.S. Publishing Co., 1970.

Corum, Ann Kondo. **Ethnic Foods of Hawai'i.** Honolulu: Bess Press, 1983.

Hirasuna, Delphine. **Flavors of Japan.** San Francisco: 101 Productions, 1981.

Itoh, Joan. **Japanese Cooking Now.** New York: Warner Books, 1980.

Junior League of Honolulu. **A Taste of Aloha.** Honolulu, 1983.

Leung, Mai. **The Classic Chinese Cook Book.** New York: Harper's Magazine Press, 1976.

Skinner, Gwen. **The Cuisine of the South Pacific.** Auckland: Hodder and Stoughton, 1983.

Solomon, Charmaine. **The Complete Asian Cookbook.** New York: McGraw-Hill, 1979.

Steinberg, Rafael. **Pacific and Southeast Asian Cooking.** New York: Time-Life Books, 1970.

A'AMA CRAB Dark-colored, fast-moving crabs that live on lava rocks next to the ocean.

A'AMA CRAB, HOW TO CATCH You'll need one bucket, one y-shaped stick or branch, some nylon

fishing line (tsuji). String the nylon line across the two branches of the y-shaped stick. Then go look for crabs. When you get close enough to an a'ama crab, quickly touch the nylon line to the crab's eye-stalks. That'll scare him and he'll pull his eyes back into his shell and the fishing line goes with them. Quickly lift him up and position him above your bucket so that he drops in.

A'AMA CRAB, HOW TO EAT You eat a'ama crab live. Turn the crab upside down and look for an upside-down "V" pointing toward the eyes. (Check for dark brown eggs along the edges of the V. If you see eggs, let the crab go because you want it to be able to lay its eggs.) Push your fingernail into the shell just above the

top of the V and pull it toward you. The meat of the crab should separate from its shell. Then rub the meat with Hawaiian salt and chew it off the shell.

ABALONE Shellfish. Usually found in supermarkets (because it doesn't grow in Hawaii).

ABURAGE (Japanese) Deep-fried tofu.

ACHIOTE BEANS OR SEEDS Dried seeds of the annatto, or lipstick tree, used in Filipino and Puerto Rican cooking to give the food a reddish-orange color. The seeds are simmered in vegetable oil or lard until the oil takes on the color from the seeds. ACHUETE in the Philippines.

ACHUETE See ACHIOTE BEANS.

ADOBO (Filipino) Braised and fried chicken or pork simmered in vinegar, garlic and spices.

AGAR-AGAR Kanten.

AHI (Hawaiian) Yellowfin tuna. Excellent for sashimi and poke, as is aku.

AHIPALAHA (Hawaiian) See ALBACORE.

AJINOMOTO Monosodium glutamate. Japanese all-purpose seasoning. Flavor enhancer.

AKU (Hawaiian) Skipjack tuna. Also known as ocean bonito. Excellent for sashimi and poke (like ahi).

FILIPINO PORK AND CHICKEN ADOBO

1 CHICKEN

1 lb. PORK

½ cup VINEGAR

2 cloves GARLIC, minced

3 BAY LEAVES

SALT and PEPPER,
   to taste

½ cup WATER

1. Cut chicken and pork into bite-size pieces.
2. Place in bowl with vinegar, garlic, bay leaves, salt and pepper. Mix thoroughly and let stand for 30 minutes.
3. Add water and cook until chicken and pork are tender. Remove from heat.
4. Remove chicken and pork pieces and fry in a little oil until well browned. Return to pot and simmer until well done.
5. Serve hot.

– Contributed by Nan Asuncion.

AKU BONE Center bone of the aku. Some consider this the best part. Often cut into sections and fried.

AKU, USES BAIT: Use belly, head, tail, bones. SOUP: Head, tail. FOR FRYING: Belly, bone, eggs. SASHIMI: Body. SHIOKARA: Guts.

AKULE (Hawaiian) Large-eyed species of Jack resembling mackerel. Try them fried, baked, smoked or dried. Baby akule are called HALALU.

ALAE SALT Hawaiian salt with a reddish color, often used at luaus. See also HAWAIIAN SALT.

ALBACORE Has the whitest flesh of any kind of tuna. Also called AHIPALAHA.

ALMOND COOKIE (Chinese) Popular giant almond-flavored cookie with a red dot in the middle.

ALMOND FLOAT

2 packages UNFLAVORED GELATIN
1 cup MILK
¾ cup SUGAR
1 tbsp. ALMOND EXTRACT
CANNED LYCHEE
CANNED MANDARIN ORANGES

1. Sprinkle 2 packages gelatin in 3 tbsp. cold water.
2. Boil 1 cup water; add gelatin mixture, stirring until dissolved.
3. Add milk, sugar and extract.
4. Stir well. Pour into small square pan; refrigerate until set.
5. Cut into cubes. Mix canned lychee and syrup with drained mandarin oranges. Serve fruit over cubes. You may add other fruits in season.

– From WHERE I LIVE THERE ARE RAINBOWS by Beverly Lee.

ALMOND FLOAT (Chinese) Almond flavored gelatin, sometimes with fruit added in. Try it chilled.

AMA'AMA (Hawaiian) Mullet.

AN (Japanese) Paste usually made from azuki beans. Also known as koshian or tsubushian.

ALMOND COOKIES

1 cup FLOUR
½ cup SHORTENING
½ tsp. BAKING POWDER
Few drops YELLOW
 FOOD COLORING

1 tsp. ALMOND
 EXTRACT
1 EGG YOLK
24 BLANCHED
 ALMONDS
6 tbsp. SUGAR

1. Cream shortening with sugar and almond extract until light and fluffy.
2. Add food coloring, then work in flour which has been sifted with salt and baking powder.
3. Shape in waxpaper into roll 1 inch in diameter; chill for 1 hour.
4. Cut into ¼-inch slices. Place on greased cookie sheets, 1 inch apart, rounding the edges of the dough.
5. Beat egg yolk and water together, then brush each slice of dough with the mixture. Press an almond well into the center.
6. Bake in oven preheated to 350° for 20 minutes or at 400° for 10 minutes, until light golden brown.

– From THE GOURMET'S ENCYCLOPEDIA OF CHINESE-HAWAIIAN COOKING
by Alyce and Theodore Char.

ANDAGI Okinawan malasada.

ANPAN (Japanese) Japanese manapua with azuki beans inside. Well, not exactly, but close enough.

ARARE (Japanese) Rice cracker. Also called KAKIMO-CHI.

GRANDMA'S ANDAGI

3 cups FLOUR
1½ cup SUGAR
1 tbsp. BAKING
  POWDER

3 EGGS
1 cup MILK
OIL, heated to 350°

1. In a large bowl, combine flour, sugar and baking powder.
2. Beat eggs in a separate bowl and add milk.
3. Fold in milk mixture with dry ingredients. Do not mix too much.
4. With a teaspoon, scoop dough into the hot oil. As dough rises to the top of the oil, turn the dough around to evenly brown the andagi. Try to make perfect dough ball slightly larger than size of a golf ball.
5. Serve warm. Reheats best in microwave oven.

– Contributed by Representative Marshall Ige.

ARROZ Spanish, Puerto Rican or Filipino word for rice.

AU (Hawaiian) Swordfish.

AWA (Hawaiian) Milkfish or bangus.

AZUKI BEANS (Japanese) Small red beans used in Japanese cooking. Often boiled with sugar to make a sweet red bean paste. Used in rice cakes, shave ice, or boiled or steamed and served alone.

BACALAO (Puerto Rican) Codfish. Also spelled BA-CALHAU (Portuguese spelling).

BAGOONG (Filipino) Salty fermented fish paste used in or as accompaniment to Philippine dishes.

BAKED COCONUT MOCHI, RECIPE See MOCHI.

BAKED STUFFED EGGPLANT, RECIPE See EGGPLANT.

BALATONG (Filipino) Stew made of mungo beans, pork, onions, tomatoes, etc.

BALLOONFISH Fish that can blow up like balloon. One has more spines, one is more smooth. Also called FUGU.

BALLOONFISH, HOW TO TAKE OUT THE POISON Ask an expert.

BALUT (Filipino) Chicken embryo, boiled in the shell. Filipino delicacy.

BAMBOO SHOOT Young, tender bamboo used in

many Oriental dishes. Also called TAKENOKO (Japanese).

BANANAS, COOKING Plantains.

BANGUS (Filipino) Milkfish. Hawaiian word is AWA.

BARBECUE FRIED CHICKEN, RECIPE See CHICKEN.

BARBECUE PORK SPARERIBS, RECIPE See PORK.

HOMEMADE BEEF JERKY

1½ to 2 lbs. BEEF FLANK

1 clove GARLIC, crushed

⅓ cup SHOYU

⅛ tsp. SALT

⅛ tsp. PEPPER

1. Slice meat lengthwise, with the grain, into ¼-inch pieces.
2. Combine remaining ingredients and mix with meat strips. Let stand 15 to 20 minutes.
3. Drain and arrange in a single layer on a rack set in shallow baking pan.
4. Bake in 150° oven or at lowest oven temperature for at least 12 hours.
5. Store in airtight container.

– Contributed by Victoria Lam.

BARBECUE PORK, FILIPINO, RECIPE See PORK.

BARRACUDA Vicious fish with lotta teeth. Good eating. Hawaiian name is KAKU.

BEAN CURD Soybean curd. See TOFU.

BEAN SPROUTS Used in Oriental cooking and haole health foods. See MUNG BEANS.

BEAN SOUP, PORTUGUESE Look under PORTUGUESE.

BEEF What paniolos round up. Often encountered in beef curry, beef cutlet, pipikaula, teri beef, corned beef and cabbage, and loco-moco.

BEER Local delicacy indispensable for tailgate parties, baby luaus, beach, yardwork, and li'dat. Also a handy Christmastime curbside offering for the guy who has everything – your garbageman.

BEER BUST Popular local fund-raising event and good excuse to get pilut to da max. Usually includes plenny food and good Hawaiian entertainment.

BENTO (Japanese) Box lunch. Common ingredients are: rice, takuwan, spam, daikon, shoyu chicken, teriyaki meat, ume, vienna sausage, nori, egg, grated ginger, and for some unknown reason, green strips of plastic.

BIBINGKA Filipino pudding made of mochiko, sugar, and coconut milk, and steamed in banana leaves.

BIHON (Filipino) Rice sticks/noodles, used in pansit. Like long rice only thinner.

BITTER MELON (Balsam pear) Small pale green melon, slightly bitter but refreshingly cool. Used in lots of Filipino and Oriental dishes. The greens from bitter melon are also used in many cooked dishes. Also called FUQUA or HUQUA.

BREADFRUIT CHIPS

1 BREADFRUIT, ripe but firm

1. Peel the skin.
2. Slice breadfruit lengthwise in thin slices.
3. Deep fry in oil until crisp and golden brown.
4. Sprinkle salt on top and serve.
5. Mo' bettah you use 2 breadfruit, cuz you going run outta dis pupu real fast!

– Contributed by Steve Miller.

BLACK BEANS Fermented beans used in Chinese cooking. Made from heavily salted soybeans.

BLACK COD See BUTTERFISH.

BLACK DOG See DOG, BLACK.

BOK CHOY Chinese cabbage with white stalks and large dark-green leaves.

BONEFISH Oio.

BONELESS CHICKEN THIGHS, RECIPE See CHICKEN.

BREADFRUIT Big round seedless fruit used as vegetable or bread substitute. The pulp has a texture like bread when it's baked and roasted. It can also be used slightly immature as a starchy vegetable. Breadfruit trees originally came from Malaya. Capt. Bligh (of MUTINY ON THE BOUNTY) first introduced them to the Americas. See 'ULU, POI'ULU.

SEEMS LIKE THERE'S ONE IN EVERY CROWD!

BROILED EGGPLANT, RECIPE See EGGPLANT.

BROK' DA MOUT' (Hawaiian) Expression meaning "Delicious!" or "I hope you get some mo' dat kine, Auntie."

BULGOGI (Korean) Thin slices of beef in a spicy sauce. Korean teriyaki.

BULUK Chinese word for jabon. Also called POMELO or MARANCAS.

BUNUELOS Filipino dumplings, fried and rolled in sugar.

BURDOCK ROOT Haole name for GOBO.

BURGER, TERI, RECIPE See TERI-BURGER.

BUTTERFISH Black cod, a fatty strong-flavored fish used a lot in Japanese cooking.

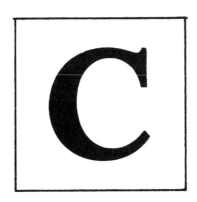

CAKES AND PIES, LOCAL FAVORITES CAKES:
Guava chiffon, haupia, passionfruit (lilikoi), coconut,
pineapple upside-down (oh yeah, and FISH). PIES:

STUFFED CABBAGE ROLLS

8 large CABBAGE
 LEAVES, parboiled
1 lb. GROUND BEEF
¼ cup SHREDDED
 CARROTS
1 ONION, chopped

1 EGG, slightly beaten
1 tsp. SALT
¼ tsp. PEPPER
1 can (10¾ oz.)
 CONDENSED TOMATO
 SOUP

1. To parboil cabbage, place cored cabbage head in
   boiling water and cook until leaves are soft and can be
   peeled off.
2. Combine all ingredients except cabbage leaves and
   soup.
3. Divide mixture among cabbage leaves.
4. Roll and secure leaves with toothpicks.
5. Place rolls in skillet.
6. Pour soup over rolls and cook over low heat for about
   40 minutes, occasionally spooning sauce over rolls.
7. Makes 4 servings.

– Contributed by Glenna Sakata.

Lilikoi chiffon, macadamia nut, banana or coconut cream, mango.

CALAMARI Another name for squid or ika.

CALIFORNIA ROLL Haole style sushi that's not rolled, it's a nori cone.

CARAMBOLA See STAR FRUIT.

CARE PACKAGES What local mothers send to the kids on the mainland. Common ingredients include: saimin, frozen laulau, crack seed, kakimochi, Maui potato chips, dried squid, abalone, Hinode rice and rice cooker, Saloon Pilot crackers, ajitsuke nori, and li'dat.

CARNE DE VINHA D'ALHOS See VINHA D'ALHOS.

CELERY CABBAGE See WON BOK.

CELLOPHANE NOODLES See LONG RICE.

CHAP CHAE, CHAP CHYE (Korean) Stir-fried dish of meat, vegetables, and noodles.

CHAR SIU (Chinese) Marinated pork with a sweet

spicy flavor. Reddish pink. Often found in saimin, but they don't put as much in as they used to.

CHAR SIU BAO (Chinese) Dumpling with char‑siu filling. Also called MANAPUA.

CHAR SIU FILLING FOR MANAPUA, RECIPE See MANAPUA.

CHAR SIU FUN Look Fun.

CHAWAN Rice bowl.

CHICHARRONES (Puerto Rican) Deep-fried pork rind.

CHICHIDANGO Variety of Japanese mochi.

CHICKEN Extremely useful local food. See also EGGS.

CHICKEN, GINGER, RECIPE See GINGER.

BARBECUE FRIED CHICKEN

2 pkg. 22 oz. FROZEN CHICKEN
4 tbsp. FLOUR
8 tbsp. CORN STARCH
¼ cup BROWN SUGAR
1 tbsp. SALT

2 EGGS
2 tbsp. OYSTER SAUCE
2 tbsp. KETCHUP
½ cup GREEN ONIONS, chopped
OIL for frying

1. Combine all ingredients with chicken.
2. Soak for three hours or overnight. Mix periodically.
3. Deep fry in oil.
4. Tastes better cooled.

– Contributed by Senator Patsy K. Young.

CHICKEN LONG RICE

2 bunches LONG RICE
3 lbs. CHICKEN, cut
  into pieces
2-inch piece GINGER,
  sliced or peeled or
  crushed

2 tbsp. SHOYU
1 tsp. MSG
4 tbsp. LIQUOR
1 tbsp. HAWAIIAN SALT
2 large ROUND ONIONS,
  sliced
2 tbsp. OIL

1. Soak long rice in water.
2. Soak chicken pieces in shoyu, MSG, ginger, liquor and salt for about 20 minutes.
3. Brown chicken in oil.
4. Brown onions.
5. Put long rice, chicken and onions in pot. Cover with chicken broth.
6. Simmer until long rice is tender.
7. Note: If using canned chicken broth and water, use less salt. Add 6 green onion stalks, cut into one-inch lengths, during last few minutes of simmering, to add color.

– From WHERE I LIVE THERE ARE RAINBOWS by Beverly Lee.

CHICKEN KATSU (Japanese) Chicken cutlet. See KATSU.

CHICKEN KATSU, RECIPE See KATSU.

CHICKEN, LEMON-SHOYU See SHOYU.

CHICKEN LONG RICE Chicken dish made with transparent noodles (long rice).

BONELESS CHICKEN THIGHS

3½ lbs. BONELESS
 CHICKEN THIGHS,
  cut into bite-size pieces
¼ cup FLOUR
½ cup CORNSTARCH
¼ cup SUGAR
1½ tsp. SALT

1 tbsp. plus 2 tsp. SHOYU
Pinch of AJINOMOTO
2 EGGS
3 stalks GREEN ONION,
 chopped
2 cloves GARLIC, minced
3 tbsp. SESAME SEED

1. Mix all ingredients and refrigerate overnight.
2. Deep-fry.

– Contributed by Glenna Sakata.

CHICKEN LUAU (Hawaiian) Chicken and coconut milk cooked in taro leaves. See LUAU, PALUSAMI.

CHICKEN MARUNGAY (Filipino) Chicken stew made with leaves of horseradish tree, garlic, ginger, and onions (optional: green papayas and tanglad). Also called KALAMUNGAY.

CHICKEN, PANKO (FLOUR), RECIPE See PAN-KO.

CHICKEN PAPAYA STEW (Filipino) Made from green papaya and chicken. Good to eat when you hapai 'cause going give you more milk.

CHICKEN, SESAME SEED, RECIPE See SESAME SEED CHICKEN.

CHIKUWA (Japanese) Round fishcake with hole in the middle.

CHILI OIL A cooking oil seasoned with red chili peppers. Better if aged.

CHILI PEPPER, HAWAIIAN (1) Chili pepper grown by a Hawaiian. (2) Small orange-red fruit used as a spicy seasoning.

CHILI RICE Chili on top of rice. Local favorite.

CHILI SPAGHETTI Chili on top of spaghetti noodles. Usually comes with macaroni salad and white bread. Another local favorite.

CHILI WATER, CHILI PEPPER WATER Water or vinegar flavored with red chili peppers and aged.

CHINESE CABBAGE Bok choy.

CHINESE PARSLEY Aromatic herb of the parsley family. Much more pungent than the regular kind of parsley. Also called CORIANDER.

CHIPS, BREADFRUIT, RECIPE See BREADFRUIT.

CHIPS, COCONUT, TOASTED, RECIPE See COCONUT CHIPS.

BRETT'S INCREDIBLE CHILI CON CARNE HAWAIIAN-STYLE

2 strips BACON
¼ cup OLIVE OIL
1 lb. GROUND ROUND
1 lb. ROUND STEAK
1 lb. CHUCK STEAK
½ lb. PORTUGUESE SAUSAGE
½ lb. KALUA PIG
8 buds GARLIC
2 ONIONS, chopped
1 rib CELERY, sliced
1 RED BELL PEPPER, diced
1 can BUDWEISER
1 can CHICKEN BROTH
2 FRESH TOMATOES, diced
½ lb. SHARP CHEDDAR CHEESE
1 FRESH LEMON
¼ block COOKING CHOCOLATE
½ can BLACK OLIVES, pitted
1 large can TOMATILLOS

1 can RED CHILI SAUCE
1 can GREEN ENCHILADA SAUCE
1 jar ARTURO'S MAUI SALSA
½ can JALAPENOS
1 can GREEN CHILES
½ cup SHOYU
2 cans TOMATO SAUCE
1 can TOMATO PASTE
2 cans STEWED TOMATOES
1 bottle CHILI POWDER
3 BAY LEAVES
1 tbsp. HAWAIIAN ROCK SALT
1 tbsp. BLACK PEPPER
⅓ bottle NIOI CHILI PEPPER WATER
1 tsp. KIAWE HONEY
½ cup MASA FLOWER (Safeway)
2 tbsp. CUMIN
1 tsp. THYME
1 tbsp. SPIKE
1 tbsp. OREGANO

(Continued)

CHIPS, POTATO, WHERE FROM Local potato chips no ka oi! And they come from Maui, Hilo, Kona, and Kauai.

CHIPS, TYPES Potato, taro, banana, breadfruit, shrimp, won ton pi, coconut, and cow.

CHINESE PICKLED VEGETABLES

6 large CUCUMBERS or
 KAI CHOY
Fresh GINGER
1½ cup SUGAR

¼ cup (less if desired)
HAWAIIAN SALT
1 cup JAPANESE
 VINEGAR

1. For cucumbers, cut into ½ inch pieces. For kai choy, cut into 1-inch pieces, trimming off some of the leaves.
2. Add a few slices of ginger, cut into strips.
3. Add Hawaiian salt. Let stand for several hours, rinse and drain.
4. Boil vinegar and sugar. Cool and pour over vegetables.

– From WHERE I LIVE THERE ARE RAINBOWS by Beverly Lee.

CHIRASHI (Japanese) Type of sushi that's more like a Japanese rice salad. Rice mixed with seafood and vegetables. Looks like mazegohan. See also SUSHI.

CHOCOLATE MEAT See DINUGUAN.

CHORIZO A hot and spicy, hard Portuguese sausage which comes in a can.

CHOW FUN Chinese dish made with fat, flat rice flour noodles. See also FUN, LOOK FUN.

CHOW MEIN (Chinese) Flat, skinny noodles.

CHOY SUM (Chinese) Greens – can be steamed or parboiled in sesame seed oil and oyster sauce or shoyu, or used in soup.

CHUN (Korean) Korean tempura. See MEAT JUN, MEAT CHUN.

CHUNG CHOI (Chinese) Salted turnip greens. Sometimes mixed with pork hash and cooked.

CHUTNEY Spicy relish usually served with curry. Mango chutney is a local favorite.

CITRONELLA See LEMON GRASS, TANGLAD.

CLAM DIP See DIP.

COCONUT Seed of the coconut palm. See also SPOON MEAT, KAHOOLAWE COCONUT.

COCONUT, EVERYTHING YOU EVER NEEDED TO KNOW ABOUT:

How to husk: Plant a stick or the back end of a pickaxe into the ground with the pointed end up. Grab the coconut with both hands and drive the coconut into the pointed stick or pick. Then pull the coconut toward you and that should remove part of the husk. (NOTE: This takes some strength.) Continue the process until the whole husk is removed. As you get closer to the hard inner shell, you may be able to pull the husk off with your hands.

How to get the juice: First look for the three "eyes" of the coconut, three indentations in the shell which form a triangle. Drill a hole with a drill or pound hole with hammer and nail, through one of the "eyes". Then insert a straw and drink the juice – or just turn upside down and let the juice come out into your mouth or a bowl.

How to crack: Take something hard, like a rock, and firmly tap the center of the triangle formed by the three "eyes". As the shell begins to crack, continue around the shell until it splits completely in half.

How to milk: Start with the grated flesh of the coconut (coconut meat), then you put the meat inside the fibrous inner husk you took off from the outer shell, and squeeze it to strain out the milk. (You can also use cheesecloth to strain the milk.)

How a Mainland City Looks to
a Hungry Local

COCONUT MOCHI, BAKED, RECIPE See MO-
CHI.

COCONUT PUDDING See HAUPIA.

COFFEE, KONA Coffee from Kona.

CONE SUSHI (Japanese) Style of sushi wrapped in

cone of aburage. In cone sushi, the rice contains bits of minced vegetables. Also called inari sushi. See also SUSHI.

COOKIE, ALMOND, RECIPE See ALMOND COOKIE.

COOKIES, LOCAL, WHERE FROM Hilo: Robert's cookies. Kauai: Tip Top cookies and Kauai cookies. Mountain View: Rock cookies.

TOASTED COCONUT CHIPS

1 fresh COCONUT, husked
SALT

1. Remove meat from fresh coconut and slice paper thin with a knife or potato peeler.
2. Spread on cookie sheet and sprinkle with salt.
3. Bake at 300° until golden brown, stirring twice to ensure even cooking.
4. Cool and store in airtight container.

– Contributed by Reiko Ibano.

CORIANDER See CHINESE PARSLEY.

COW TONGUE Used in sandwiches, roasts, teriyaki, soup, stew.

CRAB, IMITATION Fishcake masquerading as crab.

CRAB, VARIETIES Samoan, Haole, a'ama, sand, 7-11, sand turtles, hermit, white, blue pincher, Hawaiian, rock, box, Kona.

CRACK SEED (1) Preserved fruits; Chinese candy. (2) Preserved prune with a cracked seed.

CRACK SEED, HOW TO MAKE First, clean your floor. Put the prune on top da floor. Smash 'em with your hammer. Soak 'em in the sauce. If you no mo' da sauce, try buy 'em from da supahmocket.

CREAM CHEESE KAIWI, LICHEE, RECIPE See LICHEE.

CRISPY GAU GEE, RECIPE See Gau Gee.

CRISPY TAKUWAN, RECIPE See Takuwan.

CURRY Blend of spices originally from India, usually served with rice and a base of meat, fish, eggs, vegetables or whatevahs.

Hawaii's First
Inter-Island Dinner Service

CURRY STEW Stew with curry powder in it. Popular local plate-lunch item.

CUTTLEFISH Similar to squid. Available fresh, frozen or dried. Best eaten in the early morning when your breath already stinks.

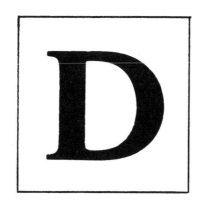

DAIKON (Japanese) Common ingredient in Japanese cooking. It's in the turnip family but tastes more like radish.

DANGO (Japanese) Dumpling. See CHICHIDANGO.

DARAAN-DARAAN See DINUGUAN.

DASHI (Japanese) Seasoned soup base. See HONDA-SHI.

DIGGING NOSE, WHEN OKAY TO When you eating saimin and you sneeze and you get one noodle up your nose.

DIM SUM (Chinese) Heavy Chinese pupus. Noodles and tea and all kine dim sum make a good lunch.

DIM SUM, VARIETIES Pepeiao, half moon, taro cake, gin dui, pork hash, rice cake, har gau, and all kinds of baked, steamed bao, including manapua.

DINADARAAN (Filipino) Another name for DINU-GUAN.

KIM CHEE DIP

1 bottle WON BOK KIM CHEE
2 blocks PHILADELPHIA CREAM CHEESE

1. Remove juice from kim chee and set aside for later.
2. Put kim chee in blender, blend on medium until kim chee texture is like a rough paste.
3. In large bowl, combine soft cream cheese and kim chee paste. Mix well.
4. For more flavor and softer dip, pour in desired amount of kim chee juice.

– Contributed by Randy Chun.

DINENGDENG (Filipino) Vegetable soup seasoned with bagoong.

DINUGUAN (Filipino) Made by sauteing meat, then simmering in vinegar mixture with seasonings (especially hot pepper). Coagulated blood is added and stirring and cooking is continued for a few minutes. Also called DINADARAAN, DARAAN-DARAAN, or CHOCOLATE MEAT.

DIP, CLAM, HOW TO MAKE You need sour cream, lemon juice, clams, salt and pepper. Put sour cream in bowl, add clams, then the lemon juice, and put salt and pepper (and chopped green onions or chives or garlic, if you like).

DOG Popular luncheon item with the ancient Hawaiians.

DOG, BLACK Popular luncheon item with Filipinos.

DOLPHINFISH Another name for MAHIMAHI.

DONBURI (Japanese) Rice dish with various toppings. Literally means "big bowl". See also OYAKO DONBURI.

DRAGON EYE Fruit resembling lichee. Chinese word for it is LONGAN (pronounced LOONG-ahn).

EBI (Japanese) Dried shrimp used in soups and other dishes.

EGGS Very young chickens. A versatile and useful food.

EHU (Hawaiian) Variety of snapper closely related to onaga.

ENSAIMADA Filipino pastry; sugar-coated roll.

ESCABECHE Fish steamed with slivers of ginger and onion.

SIMPLE BROILED EGGPLANT

¼ cup FLOUR
1 medium EGGPLANT, cut into ½-inch slices
¼ lb. BUTTER

1. Flour each eggplant slice; place on baking sheet.
2. Dot each with butter, using half of butter.
3. Broil in oven for 5 minutes.
4. Turn slices and dot with remaining butter.
5. Season to taste.

– Contributed by Glenna Sakata.

BAKED STUFFED EGGPLANT

1 large, round
  EGGPLANT
½ cup MUSHROOMS,
  chopped fine
½ cup ONION, minced
BACON, fried and
    chopped

⅓ cup BACON DRIPPINGS
1 pkg. BREAD STUFFING
¼ cup KETCHUP
2 EGGS, slightly beaten
¼ cup WATER

(Continued)

1. Cut eggplant lengthwise into 4 pieces. Cut in half to create 8 pieces. Remove pulp and cut into cubes.
2. Parboil eggplant shells for 5 minutes.
3. Cook the cubed pieces, mushrooms, and onion in bacon drippings until tender.
4. Combine bread stuffing with cooked eggplant-onion mixture, fried bacon pieces, catsup, eggs and water.
5. Stuff eggplant shells.
6. Bake in shallow pan at 350° for 30 minutes.

– Contributed by Glenna Sakata.

FILIPINO BARBECUE PORK, RECIPE See PORK.

FILIPINO PORK AND CHICKEN ADOBO, RECIPE See ADOBO.

FINGERS, EATING WITH It's okay to eat with your fingers in certain local situations like: eating poi, pupu parties, luaus, sushi, chicken (of course), malasadas, Filipino food (if traditional), shishkebab, an' when yo' moddah not looking.

FISH, DRIED Fish that are dried in the sun. Fish most commonly prepared in this way are: opelu, akule, aku, marlin, ahi, etc.

FISHCAKE (Japanese) Pureed steamed loaf of whitefish. Raw fishcake is a pinkish-brown paste. You can buy it that way in meat markets and extra fresh at Oahu Market in Chinatown. Also called KAMABOKO. See also CHIKUWA.

FILIPINO SILVERWARE...

FISHHEAD What you use (often along with bones of the fish) to make soup stock for Oriental clear broth (like for miso, saimin, etc.). Good for crab bait too. See AKU, USES.

FISH SAUCE See PATIS, BAGOONG, HARM HAR, NUOC MAM.

FIVE SPICE POWDER A must for Chinese cooking. Combination of star anise, cloves, fennel, cinnamon, peppercorns.

FLOAT, ALMOND, RECIPE See ALMOND FLOAT.

FREE PUPUS, HOW TO GET Food & New Products Show every year, go to a party where you don't know anybody and tell 'em Auntie wen invite you, go to opening of Legislature in January, look for Grand Openings of new businesses, donate blood (they give you pastries and punch), go to any non-Haole funeral.

FRITTERS, SHRIMP, RECIPE See SHRIMP FRITTERS.

FRUIT PUNCH State drink of Hawaii.

FUGU Japanese name for balloonfish. Popular delicacy in Japan. If the poison is not removed properly, it can kill you, so watch out. See also BALLOONFISH.

FUKUSA (Japanese) Style of sushi wrapped in omelette (tamago) with a little belt of nori holding it together. See also SUSHI.

FUN type of Chinese noodle. See LOOK FUN, CHOW FUN.

FUNDRAISER FOODS Foods that people sell to make money for their groups. Most common ones are: Hulihuli chicken, candy, sweet bread, Portuguese sausage, laulau, kalua pig, saimin, chili.

FUQUA Another name for BITTER MELON. Also called HUQUA.

FURIKAKE Japanese seasoning containing seaweed, salt and sesame seeds. Often encountered atop the rice in bentos.

FUT, FOODS THAT MAKE YOU Kim chee, of course; takuwan; chili; pork 'n' beans; Portuguese bean soup.

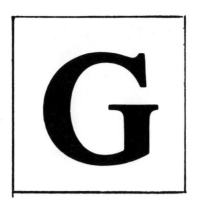

G

GAU (Chinese) Steamed sweet rice cake. Pake families always make it at Chinese New Year's. Great fried in a little oil or on non-stick pan without oil, when it hardens.

CRISPY GAU JEE or GAU GEE

2 lbs. FRESH PORK, ground
½ lb. HAM, chopped
10 medium MUSHROOMS, soaked and cleaned
14 WATER CHEST-NUTS, preferably imported
2 cans (6⅞ oz.) JAPANESE CLAMS or 1½ lbs. SHRIMP
2 EGGS, slightly beaten
1 tbsp. BROWN SUGAR
1 tsp. SALT
Dashes of PEPPER
2 tbsp. OYSTER SAUCE
1 cup GREEN ONIONS, cut fine
2 tsp. SESAME OIL
1 tsp. TAPIOCA STARCH
2 lbs. GAU JEE SKINS
OIL for deep-frying
CORNSTARCH

1. Cut mushrooms into small bits. Pare water chestnuts and cut small.
2. Cut clams into small bits and sprinkle with little pepper. If shrimps are used, shell, de-vein and cut into bits.
3. Mix all ingredients together, except Gau Jee, oil and cornstarch. Add 1 tbsp. clam juice and tapioca starch. (Save remaining clam juice for soup stock.)
4. Mix cornstarch with water to make smooth, soft paste for sealing agent.
5. Place 1 heaping tsp. of filling on one half of Gau Jee skin; fold other half over filling and seal with corn-starch paste. Turn corners of sealed edge down and place on baking sheet. Continue procedure.
6. Heat oil in skillet to 375°. Fry panful of Gau Jee at a time, not more than 1½ minutes on each side.

– From THE GOURMET'S ENCYCLOPEDIA OF CHINESE-HAWAIIAN COOKING by Alyce and Theodore Char.

GAU GEE, CRISPY Deep-fried pork-filled Chinese dumplings. Strictly local. Our friend Randall Chun tells us Chinese restaurants on the Mainland will look at you real funny if you try to order this.

GINGER Plant whose hot spicy root is used in lots of local recipes. Originally came from China but was known to the ancient Greeks.

GINGER, HOW TO KEEP FRESH Whole ginger root will keep for a few weeks wrapped in paper towels in the refrigerator. Peeled, sliced fresh ginger root, placed in a jar of dry sherry and refrigerated, can be kept for several months without losing or changing its flavor.

GISANTIS (Filipino) Stew with green peas, bamboo shoots, tomato sauce, and chicken or pork.

GOATFISH See KUMU.

GOBO (Japanese) Burdock root, often sliced into slivers and made into kimpira, or added to vegetable dishes such as nishime. Has a slightly tangy taste.

GOHAN Japanese word for rice. Refers to cooked rice.

GOMA (Japanese) Sesame seed. Called JEE MAH in Chinese. See SESAME SEED.

GOURMET PUPUS Any local pupu served on a real plate.

GRANDMA'S ANDAGI, RECIPE See ANDAGI.

GREEN PAPAYA Good in Chicken Papaya Stew.

GRINDS Local slang for FOOD. See also KAU-KAU.

GUAVA Fruit of guava tree with lots of seeds and strong smell. Usually found smashed on trails in the mountains. Used in preserves and juice – and guava chiffon cake!

GUAVA JAM (1) Local favorite topping for toast, muffins, biscuits, etc. (2) Old Sunday Manoa album.

GUINATAAN (Filipino) Sweet dessert made from coconut milk, yams, taro and bananas. Also, main dishes such as chicken, pork or fish cooked in coconut milk.

Thanksgiving, Japanese Style

HALALU (Hawaiian) Baby akule.

HALO-HALO Filipino liquid dessert of milk, ice, sugar and various fruits, like jackfruit, bananas, etc. (you can

HAMBURGER ON HASU

2 lbs. HASU, peeled
1 lb. HAMBURGER
1 tsp. SALT
¼ tsp. PEPPER
⅛ tsp. AJINOMOTO
¼ tsp. SESAME OIL

¼ cup GREEN ONION,
  chopped
Dash of GARLIC POWDER
3 tbsp. SHOYU
4 EGGS, beaten
1-2 cups FLOUR

1. Slice hasu into ¼-inch thicknesses.
2. Mix all other ingredients, except eggs and flour.
3. Spread 1-2 tsp. of hamburger mixture on each side of hasu.
4. Roll in flour, dip in beaten eggs and fry.

– Contributed by Gail Haruki who says she stole it from Joyce Fujimoto.

---

use fruit cocktail, too). Like a shave-ice with fruit and milk underneath.

HAMBURGER, LOCAL USES OF Teri-burger, loco-moco, teriyaki meatballs.

HAPUU Hawaiian tree fern.

HARM HAR (Chinese) Seasoning made of fermented shrimp. Also known as HUM HA.

HARM HAR FRIED RICE Same as regular fried rice except instead of using oyster sauce, use harm har. (And char siu, green onions, spam, whatevers, like regular fried rice.)

HASU Japanese vegetable. It's like a root, about so big.

HASU, HAMBURGER ON, RECIPE See **HAMBURGER.**

HAUPIA (Hawaiian) Coconut pudding.

HAUPIA

3-5 cups FRESH COCONUT, grated, enough to yield 3 cups of coconut milk

2 cups BOILING WATER

5½ tbsp. CORNSTARCH
4½ tbsp. SUGAR
1 tsp. VANILLA
⅛ tsp. SALT

1. Pour boiling water over grated coconut and let stand 15 minutes. Strain through pot strainer cloth or two thicknesses cheesecloth, twisting cloth and squeezing out as much milk as possible.
2. If this does not yield 3 cups coconut milk, pour enough boiling water over coconut and squeeze through cloth again, or add coconut water from coconut itself, if whole coconut is used.
3. Mix cornstarch, sugar, salt and coconut milk and boil, stirring constantly, until thickened. It should be free of lumps and should flow like molasses but slightly thinner. Use egg beater to smooth out lumps; add vanilla.
4. Pour into shallow pans; let cool. Refrigerate to set.
5. Cut into 2-inch cubes and serve on squares of ti leaves or in fluted paper cupcake containers.

– From THE GOURMET'S ENCYCLOPEDIA OF HAWAIIAN-CHINESE COOKING
by Alyce and Theodore Char.

HAWAIIAN SALT Coarse rock salt from the ocean. See also ALAE SALT.

HAWAIIAN STYLE CHILI, RECIPE See CHILI.

HERRING See KAZUNOKO.

HIBACHI Brazier. Handy Japanese cooking implement.

HONDASHI Dried bonito and kelp-based stock (like Japanese bouillon). A must for fast miso—or any kind of Oriental soup, even saimin. (But a real purist will use fish head every time.)

HOI SIN Sweet, spicy reddish-brown sauce made from soybeans, garlic and spices. Used in barbecued pork dishes and as a dip.

HULI-HULI CHICKEN Chicken grilled over kiawe coals. "Huli" is Hawaiian for "flip over" and that's how you do it.

HULI-HULI PIG See LECHON ASADO.

HUM HA See HARM HAR.

HUQUA Another name for BITTER MELON. Also called FUQUA.

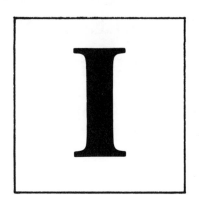

IKA (Japanese) Squid. Also called CALAMARI.

IMU (Hawaiian) Underground oven. Samoans call it UMU.

INAMONA (Hawaiian) Kukui nut paste used in poke.

INARI (Japanese) See CONE SUSHI.

IRIKO (Japanese) Small dried sardines.

JABON Japanese for pomelo. Also called BULUK, MARANCAS.

JACKFRUIT See SOURSAP.

JACKS, VARIETIES Ulua, papio, akule, halalu, pa'a'a, big-eyed scad, aji, opelu, mackerel scad.

JAI (Chinese) Monk's food. Vegetable dish eaten at Chinese New Year's.

JAMS, LOCAL VARIETIES Guava, lilikoi, mango, papaya, pineapple, poha.

JAPANESE RESTAURANT FOOD Looks pretty, which disguises the fact that there isn't enough.

JEE MAH (Chinese) Sesame seed. Japanese call it GOMA. See SESAME SEED.

JERKY, HOMEMADE BEEF, RECIPE See BEEF JERKY.

JOOK Another spelling of JUK.

JUK (Chinese) Rice soup often made with Christmas leftovers.

JUK, HOW TO MAKE Cook rice in large pot. Add water or tea, and boil. Then you add char siu, chicken or turkey meat or bone, ham or other meat, and just about anything else that feels appropriate. Serve with your choice of the following: Chinese parsley, chives, green onions, nuts, mint, chopped lettuce, Chinese fishcake.

K

KAGUMA (Japanese) Young tender shoot of Hawaiian tree fern. used in Japanese dishes like sukiyaki, miso, etc. See TREE FERN, HAPUU.

KAHOOLAWE COCONUT Hard, explosive fruit

found scattered on the island of Kahoolawe. Not recommended for consumption.

KAI CHOY (Chinese) Mustard cabbage.

KAKIMOCHI (Japanese) Rice crackers. Same as arare.

KAKU (Hawaiian) Barracuda.

KALAMANSI Filipino lime. Also refers to a seasoning made with the seeds of the kalamansi.

KALAMUNGAY See MARUNGAY, CHICKEN MA-RUNGAY.

KAL BI Spicy Korean short ribs.

KALUA PIG (Hawaiian) Imu-baked pig, often served shredded and salted.

KALUA PIG, HAOLE STYLE Bake the pork in your General Electric stove covered with banana leaves and use Liquid Smoke.

KAMABOKO See FISHCAKE, CHIKUWA.

KAMABOKO SLIPPERS See ZORIS.

KAMPYO (Japanese) Dried pulp of bottle gourd; used in making sushi.

KANG JANG Korean shoyu.

KANTEN (Japanese) Seaweed gelatin dessert. Also called AGAR-AGAR.

KAPU What you write on top of food in da refrigerator when you no like somebody else cockaroach 'um.

KARAI WATER See CHILI WATER.

KARI-KARI (Filipino) Beef and vegetable stew.

KATSU (Japanese) Chicken or pork cutlet coated with potato starch or flour. Japanese version of haole "Breaded Cutlet". See also TONKATSU, CHICKEN CUTLET. One source says the word 'katsu' comes from how Japanese pronounce the word 'cutlet'.

CHICKEN KATSU

1 box CHICKEN
SALT and PEPPER or
 AJINOMOTO, to taste
1 beaten EGG

OIL for frying
1 FRESH LEMON
¼ cup KETCHUP

1. Dice chicken into bite-size pieces.
2. Season with salt and pepper and, if you desire, ajinomoto.
3. Dip in beaten egg. Option: add water or milk to egg.
4. Pan fry until golden brown.
5. Mix juice from lemon and ketchup to make dipping sauce.

– Contributed by Dennis Fujitake.

KATSUOBUSHI (Japanese) Fish-flavored seasoning made of dried bonito flakes.

KAU-KAU Old-fashioned local way of saying GRINDS.

KAVA Shrub whose dried roots are used to make a kind of liquor. Also called 'kava-kava'. Comes from the Tongan word for "bitter". See also PUPU.

KAZUNOKO (Japanese) Herring eggs, ono over hot rice.

KIAWE CHICKEN Another name for Huli-huli Chicken – but gotta use kiawe charcoal!

KILAW (Filipino) Salad made with fish soaked in lemon juice.

KIM CHEE Korean pickled cabbage, cucumber, turnip, etc. Koreans eat it in saimin and almost everything else; practically everybody eats it with stew and rice. Gives you bad breath that will kill small animals.

KIM CHEE DIP See DIP, KIM CHEE.

KIMPIRA (Japanese) Hot vegetable dish made of gobo, shoyu and sugar (and chili pepper – optional). Also known as KIMPIRA GOBO.

KINAKO (Japanese) Ground, roasted soybeans. You roll mochi in it to add flavor.

KIWI FRUIT Fruit of a climbing shrub originally from China, now grown commercially in New Zealand. Small fruit with light-brown fuzzy skin and sweet, juicy, pale-green pulp. Kind of expensive.

KOCHU JANG (Korean) Thick, dark reddish-brown colored hot sauce. Sometimes with sesame seeds. Ono with Meat Chun.

KOKEE PLUM Sweet, juicy plum from Kokee, Kauai. Sometimes used to make ume.

KOKO See TSUKEMONO.

KONBU (Japanese) Type of seaweed.

KONNYAKU (Japanese) Clear gelatin-like blocks or noodles made from a tuber called 'devil's tongue'. Also called SHIRATAKI.

KOOK SOO (Korean) Noodles in broth, served hot or cold and garnished with meat and vegetables.

KOREAN RICE WITH BEEF, RECIPE See RICE.

KOREAN TERIYAKI SAUCE, RECIPE See TERI-YAKI.

KOREAN WATERCRESS SALAD, RECIPE See NAMUL.

KUKUI NUT PASTE See INAMONA.

KULOLO (Hawaiian) Steamed taro pudding.

KUMU (Hawaiian) Red fish with delicate white flesh. Expensive – but so ono, especially steamed with shoyu, ginger and green onions! Also called GOATFISH.

KUPIPI (Hawaiian) Small shellfish found on lava rocks in the ocean. Also called TSUBU or PIPIPI.

KUPIPI, HOW TO EAT Boil for 3-5 minutes in lightly salted water. (Can add sesame seed oil and/or chili pepper if you like.) Remove water and let 'em cool. With a needle, remove the hard black scale covering the meat. Then use the needle to remove the meat, and eat 'em!

KUROMAME Japanese black beans, usually eaten at New Year's.

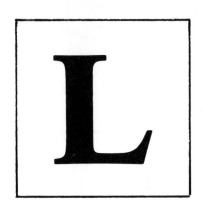

LAULAU (Hawaiian) Bundle of meat wrapped in taro leaves, then the whole thing is steamed in ti leaves. The

OVEN STYLE LAULAU

18 lbs. PORK
½ cup HAWAIIAN
  SALT
3 lbs. SALTED BUTTERFISH

10-12 lbs. LUAU LEAVES
1 cup WATER
TI LEAVES

1. Salt pork with Hawaiian salt. Cut into small pieces.
2. Cut salted butterfish into small pieces.
3. Clean luau leaves by rinsing with water. Start at stem and strip off outer membrane of each stem. Be sure to wear gloves when doing this.
4. Wrap chunks of pork and fish in luau leaves, then wrap in ti leaves. Tie with string.
5. Boil water in covered roasting pan, then place lau lau in pan. Bake at 350° for 3 hours or until leaves are soft. Repeat process until all are cooked.
6. Note: this recipe yields at least 3 dozen laulau, good for freezing or sharing with others.

– From WHERE I LIVE THERE ARE RAINBOWS by Beverly Lee.

meat can be chicken, pork or fish. Traditionally cooked in imu (ground oven).

LAULAU, HAOLE STYLE Instead of using taro leaves, wrap the meat in spinach.

LECHE FLAN (Filipino) Caramel custard.

LECHON, LECHON ASADO (Filipino) Roast suckling pig – like huli-huli pig.

LEFTOVERS Food your mother expects you to eat cold that you didn't even like hot.

LEMON GRASS Aromatic, lemon-flavored tropical grass from which you can make tea. Auntie tells us it helps her high blood pressure. Also called CITRONELLA. See also TANGLAD.

CREAM CHEESE KAIWI

1 can PITTED LICHEE
1 small block PHILADELPHIA CREAM CHEESE
1 small bottle MAUNA LOA MACADAMIA NUTS
½ cup milk

1. Mix the macadamia nuts and cream cheese and milk together, until nice and creamy.
2. Spoon the mixture into the pitted lichees

– Contributed by Brad Lum.

LOCO-MOCO

1 lb. HAMBURGER
2 cups RICE, cooked
1 pkg. HAMBURGER
  GRAVY MIX

12 EGGS
DESIRED SEASONING:
  shoyu, ketchup, etc.

1. Make 4-6 hamburger patties and fry or broil.
2. Make gravy according to instructions on package.
3. Fry eggs sunnyside up or over easy.
4. Serve 2 scoops of rice on platter; place hamburger patty on rice and 2 eggs over hamburger.
5. Pour gravy over everything and add desired seasoning.
6. Serve with desired side dish, e.g. kim chee.

– From SOMEKINE ONO COOKBOOK by Local Grines, a Junior Achievement Company.

LEMON-SHOYU CHICKEN, RECIPE See SHOYU.

LI HING MUI (Chinese) Preserved plum. Has a sweet-salty flavor.

LICHEE, LYCHEE Chinese tree grown for its fruit, which is red and ugly and poky, but inside white and soft and sweet, with a big pit.

LILIKOI (Hawaiian) Passionfruit.

LIMU (Hawaiian) Seaweed. Japanese call it OGO.

LIMU RECIPE See NAMASU, OGO.

LIMU, HOW TO PICK First you have to know (a) what edible limu looks like, and (b) which beaches have it. Then when you find a beach with lots of limu on it, you have to dig through to find the kind you can eat. Bring a

---

LOMI SALMON

1 lb. FRESH SALMON	8 GREEN ONIONS,
5 TOMATOES, peeled	chopped
and diced	1 medium ONION, chopped
	½ cup CRUSHED ICE

1. Soak salmon in cold water for 3 hours. If using frozen or canned salmon, no need.
2. Remove skin and bones and shred into fine pieces.
3. Combine all ingredients except ice, and chill.
4. Add ice just before serving, in small bowls or hollowed tomatoes.

– Contributed by Nan Asuncion.

---

big bag to put it in. And plenny suntan lotion because your back going get burned.

LINGUICA Hot, spicy Portuguese sausage.

LOCO-MOCO Complete meal in one convenient package. Rice, hamburger and egg piled one on top of the other, with brown gravy on top.

LOMI (Hawaiian) To crush, squeeze, or mash.

LOMI LOMI SALMON or LOMI SALMON Chilled fish dish of salted salmon, onion, green onion, and tomatoes. Supposedly invented by haole whalers in the early 1800's.

LONG BEANS Long beans used a lot in Filipino dishes.

LONG RICE Transparent noodles made of dried mung bean starch. Also called cellophane noodles.

LONG RICE, CHICKEN, RECIPE See CHICKEN LONG RICE.

LONGAN See DRAGON EYE.

LOOK FUN Char siu fun.

LOTUS ROOT (Chinese) Often used in soup. Can also be pickled for namasu. Good for ornamentation. Japanese call it RENKON.

LUMPIA

1 lb. HAMBURGER, CHICKEN, PORK
7 STRING BEANS, minced
3 CARROTS, shredded
¼ bag BEAN SPROUTS
1 small ONION, sliced
1 small GARLIC CLOVE, minced
SALT and PEPPER to taste
25 LUMPIA WRAPPERS

1. Brown meats and shrimp with garlic. Add onions and cook.
2. Add string beans and carrots. When vegetables are half cooked, add bean sprouts. Cook for a few more minutes, then turn off heat.
3. Spoon mixture onto lumpia wrappers, roll and seal with water.
4. Deep-fry.
5. Serve with shoyu or vinegar and garlic sauce.

– Contributed by Nan Asuncion.

LUAU Hawaiian pig-out. This word also refers to taro leaves, especially young taro tops, and the dish you make by baking taro leaves with coconut cream and chicken or octopus. See CHICKEN LUAU, PALU-SAMI, SQUID LUAU.

LUAU STEW Much like chicken luau or squid luau li'dat, except you use pork or stew meat – then you use chicken broth and luau leaves (coconut milk is optional.)

LUMPIA (Filipino) Meat (chicken, pork or beef) and vegetables wrapped in dough and deep-fried. Served with special sauce made of chopped garlic, vinegar and salt (and sometimes raisins). Lumpia is sort of a Filipino spring roll.

LUNCHWAGON Local restaurant on wheels. Usually found near the beach, near schools, construction sites, fishing spots, and so forth. Basically anywhere where there are plenty of hungry locals.

LUP CHONG, LUP CHEONG (Chinese) Small, sweet, spicy sausage. Very oily.

M

MACADAMIA NUTS Small, expensive nuts often found in cans or chocolate shells.

MAGURO Japanese word for fatty tuna.

MAHIMAHI Large white fish with delicate firm white flesh. Also known as dolphinfish (not to be confused

HONEY—I THINK THE KIDS ALREADY ATE!

with porpoise). No need say it twice when ordering in restaurants. Just say, "I like da MAHI, yeah?"

MAIS FICA Portuguese expression used when you offer food to someone and they say no. Means "Good! More fo' me!"

MAKI Style of sushi rolled in nori. Local style has tuna inside. Full name is norimaki. See also SUSHI.

MALASADA Portuguese sugar-coated donuts with no hole. Often found at Leonard's, or the red-and-white trucks you see all over the place.

MALASADAS

2 pkgs. YEAST
2 tbsp. SUGAR
⅓ cup WARM WATER
3 lbs. or 12 cups FLOUR
1 tsp. SALT
1 cup SUGAR

6 EGGS, at room temperature, slightly beaten
¼ cup BUTTER, melted
1 tsp. LEMON EXTRACT
3½ cups WARM MILK
OIL for frying

1. Mix yeast with 2 tbsp. sugar and warm water; set aside while you sift flour, salt and 1 cup sugar.
2. Add yeast mixture, eggs, butter and extract to the sifted ingredients. Mix, adding milk gradually. Knead well.
3. Cover dough and let rise 1 hour or until the dough doubles in size. Knead 2 or 3 times, if dough is to be cooked later.
4. Drop pieces of dough in heated oil and brown on both sides. Roll in sugar if desired.

– Contributed by Pris Fujioka and the Ahn Family.

CHAR SIU FILLING
FOR MANAPUA

2 cups diced CHAR SIU
1 bundle CHINESE
  PARSLEY, chopped
½ cup GREEN
  ONIONS, chopped
2 tbsp. SHOYU

1 tsp. SAKE
3 drops RED FOOD
  COLORING
1 tsp. SALT
2 tsp. RED BEAN SAUCE
1 tsp. SUGAR

1. Combine all ingredients.
2. Cook for 10 minutes.
3. Cool.

– From WHERE I LIVE THERE ARE RAINBOWS by Beverly Lee.

STEAMED MANAPUA

YEAST MIXTURE:
¼ tsp. HAWAIIAN
 SALT
2 tsp. SUGAR
1 package YEAST
½ cup FLOUR
1 cup WARM WATER

FLOUR MIXTURE:
8 cups FLOUR
1 tsp. SALT
⅓ cup OIL
½ cup SUGAR

RED FOOD COLORING

1. Prepare yeast mixture and let stand 1 hour.
2. Prepare flour mixture.
3. Gradually add yeast mixture to flour mixture.
4. Knead well. Let rise 1 hour.
5. Punch down and roll into 30 balls.
6. Fill with desired filling (bean paste or char siu).
7. Place on small squares of wax paper and let rise 1 hour.
8. Decorate top of manapua with dot of red food coloring.
9. Steam 15 minutes.

– From WHERE I LIVE THERE ARE RAINROWS by Beverly Lee.

MANDOO, MANDU Korean won ton filled with chopped meat, tofu and vegetables.

MANAPUA Hawaiian name for char siu bao. Comes from the Hawaiian expression *mea ono pua'a,* which means "delicious thing with pork inside."

MANGO Hawaiian fruit found in paper bags in business offices in early summer.

MANGO, VARIETIES Chinese, Common, Gouveia, Hayden, Pirie, Shibata.

MANGO, HOW TO EAT GREEN First peel off da skin, then slice. Mix vinegar, shoyu and sugar (and chili pepper if you like) together for a dipping sauce. Then dip the slices in and eat!

MANGO, HOW TO FREEZE Remove skin, slice into pieces, roll in sugar and wrap in freezer paper or put in any kind of container, then put in freezer.

MANGO, HOW TO PICK Get a mango picker. (For those of you who don't know, that's a long pole with a wire hoop and a cloth net at the end. You position the net under the mango, then jiggle the mango with the pole until it falls into the net.)

MANGO SEED Preserved mango; type of crack seed.

MANINI (Hawaiian) Small, striped surgeonfish. Has lots of bones. Best when fried or pulehu.

MANJU (Japanese) Small flaky bun filled with sweet azuki bean paste (koshian). Maui manju is a popular bring-home-from-Maui item.

MANOA LETTUCE A leafy, semi-head lettuce. When local girls make sandwiches for local boys, they better use Manoa Lettuce inside.

MARANCAS Filipino for pomelo. Also called BULUK or JABON.

MARUNGAY (Filipino) leaves of the horseradish tree. Also called KALAMUNGAY. See CHICKEN MARUNGAY.

MAUI ONIONS Sweet, mild onion grown in volcanic soil — on Maui, of course.

MAZEGOHAN (Japanese) Vinegar rice mixed with meat and/or vegetables.

McDONALD'S A restaurant whose mainland outlets do NOT serve saimin or portuguese sausage.

MEAT JUN, MEAT CHUN (Korean) Thin strips of beef fried in egg batter.

MEIN (Chinese) Noodles. Koreans call them MYUN.

MENPACHI (Japanese) Red reef fish with big round eyes. Variety of squirrelfish.

MINALI NAMUL, RECIPE See NAMUL.

MIRIN Sweet rice wine used in Japanese cooking.

MISO (Japanese) Fermented soybean paste used as soup stock or as sauce.

MISO SOUP, HOW TO MAKE Boil water. Add desired amount of miso, to taste. Garnish with green onion, fishcake, chives, spam, char siu, cube tofu, fish, nori, egg, dried shrimp, pork, noodles . . . you get the idea.

MOCHI (Japanese) Rice cake. Made from rice and glutinous rice flour called MOCHIKO.

MOCHI CRUNCH Another name for kakimochi or arare.

MOCHI, HOW TO POUND Needed: Steamed rice, mochiko, usu (mortar) and kine (mochi pounder). Pounding the mochi usually is done with two people, one using the kine (pronounced KEE-neh) to pound the steamed rice on the usu, while the other person reaches in to turn the rice so it gets pounded evenly. This is the person in danger. This person also adds water occasionally. When the rice has the consistency of dough, it's taken to a table and handfuls of it are pulled off and rolled in mochiko. Then these are shaped into little round cakes.

BAKED COCONUT MOCHI

1 lb. MOCHIKO
2 cups SUGAR
2 tsp. BAKING
 POWDER
3 cups MILK
1 block BUTTER, melted

5 EGGS, beaten
1 tsp. VANILLA
1 tsp. LEMON EXTRACT
1 pkg. COCONUT
 FLAKES

1. Blend all ingredients and pour into 9 x 13 baking dish.
2. Bake at 350° for 1 hour and 15 minutes.
3. Cool and cut into small rectangles for serving.

– Contributed by Barbara Takata.

MOCHIKO (Japanese) Glutinous rice flour.

MODERN MOCHI, RECIPE See NANTU.

MONK'S FOOD See JAI.

MOON CAKE (Chinese) Pastry with variety of fillings, including sweet-bean paste, nuts and meats, coconut and peanuts. With or without salted egg yolk in middle. Traditional food for Chinese Moon Festival in the fall.

MORCELA (Portuguese) Blood sausage.

NANTU
(Modern Mochi)

1½ cup MOCHIKO   ½ cup SUGAR
1½ cup WATER   2 drops FOOD COLORING
KINAKO

1. Mix all ingredients and pour into microwave-proof cooking dish.
2. Microwave for 9 minutes on HIGH setting.
3. Cool and cut into small rectangles.
4. Coat with kinako.

– Contributed by Gail Haruki.

MOUNTAIN APPLE Small, juicy red fruit that grows in the mountains.

MSG See AJINOMOTO.

MULLET Homely fish that tastes good. Hawaiian name is 'AMA'AMA.

MUNG BEANS, MUNGO BEANS The kind of beans that you get bean sprouts from. Also used to make long rice and pork dishes. See BALATONG.

MUSHROOM See SHIITAKE.

MUSTARD CABBAGE Kai choy.

MUSUBI (Japanese) Cooked rice shaped into triangles or balls. Sometimes get ume or other surprises inside.

MUSUBI, HOW TO MAKE Needed: Rice, salt, water, nori, ume (optional). Cook the rice with extra water and cool. Wet your hands and pour salt into your palms. Scoop the rice up in your hand and with both hands, shape it into triangles or balls, depending on the shape of your hands. Wrap in squares of nori. OPTIONAL: After scooping rice into palm of hand, place ume in middle. NOTE: There are musubi molds you can buy at the store if you no like use your hands.

MUSUBI, SPAM See SPAM MUSUBI.

MYUN Korean for MEIN (noodles).

NAMASU (Japanese) Raw vegetables marinated in a rice vinegar dressing.

MINALI NAMUL
KOREAN WATERCRESS SALAD
A Microwave Recipe

1 bunch WATERCRESS
1½ tbsp. SHOYU
1 tbsp. WHITE or
 JAPANESE RICE
 VINEGAR

¼ tsp. SESAME SEED OIL
1½ tsp. minced GREEN
 ONION
2 tsp. crushed or ground
 SESAME SEED

1. Wash the watercress and cut into 1½-inch lengths.
2. Place watercress stems along edges of a two-quart size casserole dish. Place leaves in the center and cover. Microwave for two to three minutes on high or until wilted yet crisp. Drain and cool.
3. Combine remaining ingredients and pour over watercress.
4. Toss and chill.

From ISLAND STYLE MICROWAVE COOKING by Joseph Melillo.

NAMASU, OGO, RECIPE See OGO NAMASU.

NAMASU, TYPES Cucumber, carrot, turnip (daikon), limu/ogo, onion, cabbage, bean sprout. Sometimes crab or other shellfish is added.

NAMOOL, NAMUL Korean salad. Vegetables in a sauce of sesame seeds, oil, vinegar and soy sauce.

NANTU Popular Okinawan mochi.

NIGIRI (Japanese) Style of sushi with seafood on top. See SUSHI.

NISHIME (Japanese) Cooked vegetable dish with pork or chicken.

NORI (Japanese) Sheets of dried seaweed used to wrap sushi or rice balls, or as garnish for many Japanese soup dishes (miso, saimin, somen, etc.) See SUSHI.

NORI, HOW TO MAKE CRISPY Lightly grill the nori over low heat in frying pan.

NORIMAKI (Japanese) Full name for MAKI SUSHI.

NUOC MAM Vietnamese fish sauce. Even fishier than patis, bagoong or harm har.

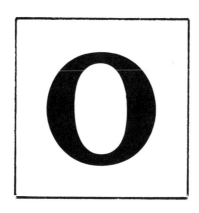

O'AMA (Hawaiian) Baby weke.

O'AMA, HOW TO CATCH, PREPARE AND EAT:
How to catch: When the o'ama are running, it's a big deal. Everybody goes to Maunalua Bay, out by Hawaii Kai. They wade out with their bamboo fishing poles, quarter-inch hooks, frozen shrimp for bait, and scoop

GEE, HONEY— HAVE I GOT THE RIGHT HOUSE? HOW COME YOU AND MOM AREN'T FIGHTING OVER WHO'S IN CHARGE OF DINNER?

nets to catch the o'ama in once they're hooked.

How to prepare: Scale and gut the fish, then soak in vinegar for at least a week. At the end of this time it should be soft enough to be eaten, bones and all. Another option is to flour it and pan-fry it.

OCHA Japanese tea.

OCHAZUKE Cooked rice, something to flavor it with, and hot tea poured over it.

OCTOPUS Tako.

OCTOPUS, HOW TO KILL You sure you want to know? Turn the head of the octopus *inside out,* then bite it. For real!

OGO Japanese word for particular type of edible seaweed. See also LIMU.

OHELO Hawaiian plant with small red or yellow edible berries. Sacred to Pele.

OIO Bonefish.

OKARA (Japanese) Tofu residue. Can be mixed with vegetables or seafood and put on top of hot rice. High in protein.

OKOLEHAO (Hawaiian) Liquor distilled from ti root; also, gin made from rice or pineapple juice.

OKRA Edible pod of okra plant. Used in soups and as a vegetable. Kinda slippery when you cook it.

OCTOPUS POKE

1 lb. OCTOPUS, cooked	1 tsp. SESAME SEEDS, toasted
1 tbsp. SHOYU	
1 tsp. SALT	1 tbsp. LEMON JUICE
1 tsp. SUGAR	½ cup OGO, chopped
	1 tsp. crushed KUKUI NUT

1. Cut octopus into bite-size pieces.
2. Mix with remaining ingredients and refrigerate for 30 minutes before serving.

Contributed by Kevin I.

OGO NAMASU

2-4 cups OGO, cleaned
¾ cup SUGAR
1¼ cup RICE (OR LIGHT) VINEGAR
1 tbsp. SHOYU
½ tsp. AJINOMOTO
1 tbsp. SESAME SEEDS

1 tbsp. GREEN ONION or ROUND ONION, sliced fine
1 tsp. SESAME SEED OIL
2 CHILI PEPPERS, seeded and chopped
2 cloves GARLIC, mashed

1. Pour boiling water over ogo. Let stand a few minutes if soft texture is desired. Remove immediately if crispier texture is wanted.
2. Rinse in cold water and drain thoroughly.
3. Pour sauce made of remaining ingredients over seaweed; place in clean jars and refrigerate.

– Contributed by Laurie Levine.

ONAGA (Japanese) Variety of red snapper. Hawaiian name is ULA ULA.

ONG CHOI Swamp cabbage.

ONION, MAUI See MAUI ONION.

ONIONS, PICKLED See PORTUGUESE PICKLED ONIONS or SABULA DE VINHA.

ONO (1) Hawaiian for "Delicious!" (2) Long skinny fish with very moist, slightly coarse white flesh. Also called wahoo.

ONO ONO SHAKES AND MALTS Special secret concoction from KC Drive-In with bananas, ice cream, peanut butter and we don't know what else. So ONO!

OPAE (Hawaiian) Baby shrimp or prawn, excellent for bait.

OPAKAPAKA (Hawaiian) Variety of blue snapper which is delicious baked, fried, broiled or as sashimi.

OPELU (Hawaiian) Species of Jack. Similar to akule.

OPIHI (Hawaiian) Small shell limpets found on ocean rocks.

OPIHI, HOW TO PICK AND EAT Pretty simple actually. Go find lava rocks near breakwater, take screwdriver or something strong to pry them off the rocks. They're dark-colored and look like little miniature volcanoes clinging to the rocks. While you're doing this, be sure to watch out for the waves. Once you've gotten the opihi off the rocks, pry them loose from their shells and pop them into your mouth.

OPU The most essential organ in the local body.

OVEN STYLE LAULAU, RECIPE See LAULAU.

OX Where oxtails are grown.

OXTAIL SOUP Popular local soup. Ingredients vary, but here's one list: oxtail, chicken stock, ginger, daikon, squash, carrots, mustard cabbage, round onion.

OXTAIL STEW Popular local stew. Like Oxtail Soup, ingredents vary, but here's our version: oxtail, onions, carrots, potatoes, cabbage, string beans, tomato sauce, and cornstarch for thickening.

OYAKO DONBURI (Japanese) Rice topped with chicken and eggs. See also DONBURI.

OYSTER SAUCE (Chinese) Seasoning made of fermented oysters.

OZONI (Japanese) Breakfast soup made from mochi and vegetables (and some people add in shellfish). Traditionally eaten on New Year's Day.

PAELLA (Puerto Rican, Filipino) Originally Spanish everything-but-the-kitchen-sink casserole featuring rice, meat, seafood, vegetables.

PALU Polynesian condiment made from chopped bits of the head and stomach of fish, mixed with kukui nut relish, garlic and chili peppers.

PALUSAMI (Samoa and throughout the Pacific) Baked parcels of taro leaves (sometimes taro, banana and breadfruit leaves are all used together) containing coconut cream. You can also include onion, chopped corned beef, prawns, any fish, fish head or entrails, or any meat or poultry. This is a universal Pacific dish, in Hawaii called LUAU. See LUAU, CHICKEN LUAU, SQUID LUAU.

PANKO Japanese flour meal to give deep-fried foods crispy texture. Like Japanese bread crumbs.

PANSIT, PANCIT (Filipino) Pork, chicken and sausage with noodles. Filipino chop suey.

PANKO (FLOUR) CHICKEN

1 box CHICKEN
 THIGHS
Favorite BARBECUE SAUCE
1 pkg. PANKO (sold in
 Japanese food section)

1 beaten EGG
OIL for frying

1. Debone chicken.
2. Soak overnight with favorite barbecue sauce.
3. Next day, roll chicken in panko, dip in egg and pan fry
    (350°) until golden brown.

– Contributed by Dennis Fujitake.

PANSIT

1 pkg. FINE NOODLES
1 tbsp. SHORTENING
1 GARLIC CLOVE,
  crushed
1 small ONION, sliced
1 lb. PORK, cubed

½ lb. SHRIMP, cut into
  bite-size pieces
1 tsp. SALT
PEPPER, to taste
CHAR SIU MEAT, sliced

1. Cook noodles in a generous amount of boiling salted water until tender; drain.
2. Heat shortening in skillet and brown garlic. Remove garlic and fry onions until partially cooked.
3. Add pork and cook until meat is tender, adding the shrimp, salt and pepper when the pork is half cooked.
4. Add noodles to pork and shrimp mixture and serve on large platter. Garnish with char siu slices.

– Contributed by Nan Asuncion.

PAO DOCE (Pronounced PAWN DOOSS) Portuguese sweet bread.

PAPAYA Pear-shaped fruit which is yellow and tender when ripe and has lots of black seeds in the center. Introduced to Hawaii in the 1880's.

PAPAYA FLOWERS Yes, you can eat them. Make a syrup of 2 cups sugar, one-half cup water, one-half cup lemon juice; when boiling, drop flowers into syrup and cook until flowers are transparent.

PAPAYA, VARIETIES Solo, Kamiya, and the red kine from Kauai.

PAPIO Young fish (under 10 lbs.) of the various species of ulua (jack).

PARTY PUPUS Two kinds:
(a) LOCAL: Won ton, sushi, sashimi, potato salad, macaroni salad, fried chicken, etc.
(b) HAOLE: Carrot sticks, cheese, crackers, potato chips with several kinds of dip, and tiny triangle-shaped sandwiches.

PASSION FRUIT Small tropical fruit also known as LILIKOI.

PATELE

½ to 1 bunch GREEN BANANAS
10 lbs. PORK BUTT
6 bunches CHINESE PARSLEY
10 whole GARLIC SECTIONS
5 bunches GREEN ONION
5 cans WHOLE OLIVES
½ cup PAPRIKA
¼ cup AJINOMOTO
¼ cup SALT
10 HAWAIIAN CHILI PEPPERS, minced
100 TI LEAVES
5 cups ACHIOTE BEANS
1 gallon WESSON OIL
5 whole ONIONS
¼ cup OREGANO

1. Soak unpeeled green bananas in Hawaiian salt and water. Peel, then grate bananas.
2. Boil 1 gallon Wesson oil in pot, add achiote beans until coloring of oil is dark. To test achiote oil for readiness, check achiote beans to see if they have lost

(Continued)

110

their color; they will look kind of brown. Strain oil with cloth material.

3. Add 12 dashes salt to grated bananas and add cooled achiote oil gradually, while mixing with hand. Grated banana is called the masa. Masa should be golden color.

4. Chop pork butt in small pieces, ½ inch in diameter. Dice all vegetables. Brown chopped pork. Add garlic, green onions and onions. Add salt to taste.

5. After browning, add six cups of water; bring to boil and let boil for 30 minutes. Meanwhile, add parsley, oregano, salt, paprika, minced chili pepper, and ajinomoto. Boil until water is almost gone. Add remainder of achiote oil to cooked meat and let boil for 5 minutes.

6. Strip hard bone off ti leaves. Be sure there are no tears or holes in leaves.

7. Place 2 ti leaves together.

8. Take a little bit of oil from pan and put on ti leaves, so masa won't stick.

9. Flatten masa (banana) to an oval shape and place on ti leaves.

10. Place serving of matuda (meat) on masa and place 1 or 2 olives on top.

11. Fold patele to desired size. Tie with string. Freeze or steam.

12. TO STEAM: Steam patele on high heat for 1½ to 2 hours. Be sure pateles are above water level. They taste better when steamed this way. Boiling would diminish taste.

13. Makes 50 to 100 pieces.

– Contributed by women of Hale No Na Wahine via Dana Hall.

PASTELES (Puerto Rican) Bananas stuffed with pork (and sometimes raisins). Like a sweet lumpia.

PASTELILLOS (Puerto Rican) Fried pork turnovers.

PATELE Sort of like a Latin laulau. See the recipe for more info.

PATIS Filipino fish sauce, a salty clear brownish liquid, used the way the Japanese use shoyu.

PICKLED VEGETABLES, CHINESE, RECIPE See CHINESE PICKLED VEGETABLES.

PICKLED ONIONS, PORTUGUESE, RECIPE See PORTUGUESE PICKLED ONIONS.

PIES See CAKES AND PIES, LOCAL FAVORITES.

PIG The animal that brought you pork, sausage, bacon, pig's feet soup, dinuguan, pork adobo, tonkatsu, pork chops, and a whole lot of other stuff.

PIG'S BLOOD Filipino cooking ingredient. See DINU-GUAN.

PIG'S FEET SOUP Clear broth containing pig's feet, vegetables, etc. Like oxtail soup only with pig's feet.

PINAKBET (Filipino) Cooked vegetable dish flavored with shrimp or pork, and using tomatoes, onions, garlic sauce, bagoong. Vegetables can include any kine, like eggplant, bitter melon, string beans, even potato leaves. Up to you.

PIPIKAULA Cured, dried beef. Hawaiian version of beef jerky.

PIPIKAULA RECIPE See BEEF JERKY, HOME-MADE.

PIPIPI See KUPIPI.

PLANTAIN Fancy name for cooking bananas.

PLATE LUNCH One of the few ways to satisfy a local stomach for not much money. Always on paper plates, usually with rice and/or macaroni salad or potato salad, plus the main course (see next entry).

PLATE LUNCH, KINDS Pork cutlet, beef cutlet, beef/pork/chicken teriyaki, spaghetti, chili-spaghetti, chili, seafood (shrimp, fish and scallops), Hawaiian plate (laulau, lomi salmon, poi, haupia), curry stew, beef stew, roast pork, roast beef, chicken/beef/shrimp curry, fried chicken, tonkatsu, chicken katsu, pork katsu, fried rice, fried noodles, fried saimin, pork chops, mahi, chop steak, hamburger steak, kal bi, shrimp tempura, shoyu chicken, mix plate, and probably more we didn't think of. NOTE: Plate lunches often have brown gravy over *everything*.

PLUM SAUCE Sweet, spicy sauce used as a dip at table for Chinese foods and as an ingredient in Chinese cooking. Made from plums, chilies, vinegar, spices and sugar.

POCHERO Filipino casserole of meat, vegetables, chickpeas and sweet potatoes.

POHA Hawaiian word for cape gooseberry or ground cherry. Makes great jam.

POI (Hawaiian) Steamed taro root which is then pounded until it's a paste. Staple food of old Hawaii.

POI, HOW TO PREPARE AND EAT THE STORE-BOUGHT KIND: Go to the supermarket and buy a plastic bag that says "Poi" on it. Then go home and squeeze out the contents of the bag into a big bowl. Then add water and stir. Depending on the amount of water you add, you get different consistencies. More water: two-finger or three-finger poi. Less water: one-finger poi. NOTE: You can buy fresh or day-old (or two- or three-day old) poi. The older the poi, the more sour. Some people like it fresh, some like it sour.

POI 'ULU Breadfruit poi – paste made from breadfruit in the same way as the Hawaiians use taro.

PORK SINUGBA or FILIPINO BARBECUED PORK

2 lb. PORK
1 small ONION
2 medium RIPE
  TOMATOES
⅓ cup WHITE VINEGAR

SALT and PEPPER, to
  taste
Pinch of AJINOMOTO and
  couple drops PATIS,
  optional

1. Cut pork into 1-inch thick steaks. Cut tomatoes into ½- to 1-inch cubes and slice onion.
2. Charcoal-broil or pan-fry pork until dark brown and almost dehydrated.
3. Cut steak into bite-size pieces and mix with tomatoes and onion and seasoning. Add more vinegar or add water to vinegar to adjust for taste.

– Contributed by Charles Roylo.

POKE (Pronounced PO-kay) In Hawaiian this word means to cut, slice, cut crosswise. So it can be applied to any kind of food prepared this way, but especially fresh, raw fish. After slicing, mix it with kukui seed paste (inamona), hot red peppers, seaweed, sesame seeds, and stuff li'dat, and eat with caution!

POKE, VARIETIES Limu poke, shoyu poke, aku poke, akule poke, marlin poke, swordfish poke, butterfish poke, tako poke, clam poke, etc.

POKE, OCTOPUS, RECIPE See OCTOPUS.

POMELO Another name for marancas, jabon or buluk (grapefruit).

PORK Very popular local food. See also PIG.

PORK AND CHICKEN ADOBO, RECIPE See ADOBO.

BARBECUE PORK SPARERIBS

1½ to 2 lbs. PORK RIBS
WATER
1 inch GINGER ROOT
SAUCE:

½ cup KETCHUP	1 tsp. GARLIC POWDER
½ cup BROWN SUGAR	1 tsp. CHILI POWDER
1 tsp. LIQUID SMOKE	1 tsp. AJINOMOTO

1. Boil pork ribs for 1½ hours in enough water to cover pork and ginger root.
2. Heat sauce.
3. Coat pork ribs with sauce.
4. Cook over barbecue.

– Contributed by Linda G. McEvoy

PORTUGUESE BEAN SOUP A staple of most local diets. Good for when you sick or late-night snack after going Cazimeros. See also FUT, FOODS THAT MAKE YOU.

PORTUGUESE PICKLED ONIONS The Portuguese call them SABULA DE VINHA.

PORTUGUESE ROAST See VINHA D'ALHOS.

PORTUGUESE SAUSAGE Very spicy pork sausage. Necessary ingredient of good Island breakfast.

POTATO Haole rice.

PORTUGUESE BEAN SOUP

½ lb. SMOKED HAM
1 PORTUGUESE
 SAUSAGE
1 cup NAVY BEANS,
 soaked overnight in
 water
1 large CARROT, cut in
 pieces

2 medium POTATOES, cut
 in pieces
1 large ONION, sliced
SALT, to taste
6 cups WATER
1 can TOMATO SAUCE

1. Boil the 6 cups of water and tomato sauce with beans
 for 1 hour or until beans are tender.
2. Add other ingredients and cook until tender.
3. Season with salt and pepper. You may add spaghetti
 or macaroni to the above for bulk.

– Contributed by Pris Fujioka and the Ahn Family.

PORTUGUESE PICKLED ONIONS

1 qt. WHITE VINEGAR
1 qt. WATER
⅓ cup HAWAIIAN
 ROCK SALT
½ cup SUGAR
4 lbs. MAUI ONIONS, quartered

2-3 large CARROTS,
 optional
1 large GREEN PEPPER,
 optional

1. Bring vinegar, water, salt and sugar to a boil.
2. Pour over onions (carrots and green pepper, if added).
3. Let cool. Refrigerate ONE MONTH before eating.

– Contributed by Pris Fujioka and the Ahn Family.

POTATO CHIPS See CHIPS.

POTATO SALAD

3 medium size
  POTATOES, cooked
  and cubed
1 MAUI ONION, minced
CELERY STALKS,
  minced
1 can TUNA, oil drained

2 cups COOKED PEAS
4-5 tbsp. MAYONNAISE
2 tsp. MUSTARD
SALT and PEPPER, to
  taste

1. Mix all ingredients, adding peas last.
2. Chill before serving.

– Contributed by Pat Sasaki.

PUDIM FLAN (Portuguese) Custard.

PULEHU Charcoal broiling, Hawaiian style.

PUPU Hawaiian word meaning PARTY GRINDS. Originally meant fish, chicken or banana served with kava.

PUPU STYLE TERI BURGER, RECIPE See TERI BURGER.

PUPUS, PARTY See PARTY PUPUS.

R

RENKON Japanese word for lotus root.

RICE Any local meal without rice is just a snack. Also called GOHAN, but only when it's cooked.

124

RICE COOKER Indispensable local household appliance.

RICE CRACKERS See ARARE, KAKIMOCHI, SENBEI.

KOREAN RICE WITH BEEF

¼ lb. GROUND BEEF
¼ lb. MUSHROOMS, sliced
3 tbsp. SHOYU
¼ cup VEGETABLE OIL
½ cup ONION, minced

2 cups COOKED RICE
¼ cup SESAME SEEDS
1 tsp. RED PEPPER, crushed
3 cups BEEF STOCK
SALT

1. Heat half of the oil in a large saucepan.
2. Add the onion, mushroom and rice. Cook over low heat for about 5 minutes. Stir constantly so the onion doesn't brown.
3. Remove from pan.
4. Put the ground beef and the rest of oil in the same pan. Cook beef until it loses its red color. Break it up as you stir so that lumps are avoided.
5. Add the shoyu, crushed pepper, beef stock and salt to taste. Add the rice and onion mixture. Stir well.
6. In the meantime, toast the sesame seeds by placing them in a shallow roasting pan in a 350° oven for about 20 minutes or until golden brown. Add toasted sesame seeds to the mixture.
7. Cover the pan, and bring to a boil. Reduce the heat and simmer for 20 minutes or until rice is tender.
8. Serves 6.

– Contributed by Gerri Kaneshiro.

RICE, FRIED Cooked rice pan-fried with meat, seafood, or vegetables and spiced (with shoyu, sesame seed oil, oyster sauce, etc.).

RICE, LONG, CHICKEN, RECIPE See CHICKEN LONG RICE.

RICE, STICKY Rice of choice for bentos and plate lunch. Also used as glue substitute in emergencies.

RICE, STYLES OF PREPARATION Japanese style is sticky. Chinese style is moist but not sticky. Haole style is fluffy (Uncle Ben's).

RICE VINEGAR Japanese vinegar; lighter and sweeter than Haole vinegar. Also called rice wine vinegar; also called mirin.

SABULA DE VINHA What the Portuguese call Portuguese pickled onions. See ONIONS, PICKLED and PORTUGUESE PICKLED ONIONS.

SAIMIN Incredibly popular noodle soup which must have been invented in Hawaii because the Chinese say THEY didn't bring it and the Japanese say THEY didn't bring it either. At any rate it's one of the few local foods that any haole from the Mainland can enjoy right away.

SAKE Japanese rice wine. Drink it hot.

SALAD, MACARONI Local staple often found in plate lunches.

SALAD, POTATO Another local staple often found in plate lunches, though not quite as often as macaroni salad.

SALAD, POTATO, RECIPE See POTATO SALAD.

SALAD, SOMEN Thin Japanese noodles garnished with fishcake, vegetables, char siu, and flavored with a sesame-oil-based sauce. See also SOMEN.

SALMON, LOMI See LOMI SALMON.

SALMON, LOMI, RECIPE See LOMI SALMON.

SALMON SUSHI, SALT, RECIPE See SUSHI.

SALT, HAWAIIAN See ALAE SALT, HAWAIIAN SALT.

SALT SALMON SUSHI, RECIPE See SUSHI.

SARDINES See IRIKO.

SARI-SARI (Filipino) Vegetables, fish and meat in a broth.

SASHIMI (Japanese) Raw salt-water fish. The way it is sliced is very important. It's the kind of pupu you take to a party if you want the host or hostess to really like you.

SATO SHOYU See SHOYU SATO.

SAUSAGE, VARIETIES Portuguese, Lup Cheong (Chinese), Blood, Pork, Chorizo, Linguica, etc. – and of course, Vienna.

SEAWEED See LIMU, OGO.

SEKIHAN (Japanese) New Year's dish made with rice and azuki beans.

SENBEI (Japanese) Sweet rice crackers.

SEQUA Type of Chinese squash. Like bitter melon, but not bitter.

SESAME OIL A cooking oil used in stir-frying (fried rice, noodles, vegetables) and other frying – enhances the flavors of foods cooked in it.

SESAME SEED Can be bought roasted or unroasted. Flavor-adding garnish used on top of lots of local foods. Called JEE MAH in Chinese, GOMA in Japanese.

SESAME SEED CHICKEN

5 lbs. CHICKEN THIGHS
GARLIC POWDER, SALT, PEPPER, to taste
1 cup POTATO STARCH
MARINADE:
½ cup WATER
¾ cup SHOYU
4 tbsp. BROWN SUGAR
4-5 stalks GREEN ONION, chopped
2 tbsp. SESAME SEEDS, toasted
2-3 tsp. grated GINGER

1. Debone chicken and cut into bite-size pieces.
2. Season to taste with garlic powder, salt and pepper.
3. Marinate chicken 2-3 hours.
4. Roll chicken pieces in potato starch.
5. Deep fry.

– Contributed by Pat Sasaki.

SHABU-SHABU (Japanese) Take meat, seafood and/or vegetables and swish them in simmering broth to partially cook them. The name "shabu-shabu" comes from the swishing sound the food makes when you're cooking it.

SHARK We haven't tried it ourselves, but we're told it tastes like swordfish. Prepare just as you would prepare any other fish.

SHAVE ICE Island tradition. Ice is shaved off a big block and put into a cone, then different flavors of syrup are poured over it.

SHAVE ICE, VARIETIES Pineapple (blue for some reason), strawberry, cherry, banana, coconut, root beer, rainbow, with azuki beans and ice cream.

SHIITAKE (Japanese) Dried black mushrooms.

SHIOKARA (Japanese) Fish guts. See AKU, USES.

SHIOYAKI Japanese way of broiling with salt. Rub salt into skin of fish (or chicken), then broil. Helps retain moisture and flavor.

SHIRA AE (Japanese) Watercress-tofu salad.

SHIRATAKI Yam noodles. See KONNYAKU.

SHOYU Soybeans, barley and salt are the main ingredients of this dark brown liquid which is always found on the table in local restaurants along with salt, pepper and sugar. Very important in Oriental cooking. Also called SOY SAUCE. Koreans call it KANG JANG.

SHOYU CHICKEN Chicken cooked in shoyu-based sauce. Very popular local dish.

SHOYU SATO Shoyu and sugar sauce in which fish, Vienna sausage, sliced hot dogs, or spam is cooked. Also known as Sato Shoyu.

SHRIMP Local crustacean who gets invited to a lot of parties. Usually seen in curry, tempura, or dim sum.

SHRIMP TEMPURA Very popular local Japanese food. See TEMPURA.

HAWAIIAN STAPLE FOOD

LEMON-SHOYU CHICKEN

1 2-3 lb. CHICKEN FRYER, cut into pieces, or 2 pkg.
  CHICKEN DRUMMETTES

MARINADE:

¼ cup OIL	½ tsp. grated GINGER
⅓ cup LEMON JUICE	1 tsp. AJINOMOTO
¼ cup SHOYU	½ tsp. SALT
2 tbsp. SUGAR	¼ tsp. PEPPER
1 clove GARLIC, crushed	

1. Marinate chicken pieces in sauce for 2-3 hours.
2. Place chicken on roasting pan rack.
3. Roast in oven at 325° for one hour, or 35-45 minutes
   for drummettes.

– Contributed by Glenna Sakata.

SIMPLE BROILED EGGPLANT, RECIPE See EGGPLANT.

SINIGANG (Filipino) Soup made with fish, shrimp or meat with vegetables and tamarind pulp. Looks sort of like a cross-section of a swamp.

SINUGBA (Filipino) Barbecued pork. See PORK, FILIPINO BARBECUED for more information.

SNAPPER, VARIETIES Ehu, kalekale, onaga, opakapaka, taape, uku.

SNOW PEAS Small, flat pods containing embryonic peas. Used in many Oriental dishes. Also known as sugar peas or Chinese peas.

SHRIMP FRITTERS

1 cup FLOUR
1 tsp. BAKING
 POWDER
1 tsp. SALT
1 tbsp. SUGAR
¼ tsp. PEPPER
OIL for frying
1 EGG

½ cup WATER
1 cup STRING BEANS,
 ROUND ONIONS,
 CARROTS, GOBO,
 GREEN ONIONS, minced
1 cup SHRIMP (½ lb.),
 minced

1. Add water to beaten egg.
2. Add to dry ingredients and mix well.
3. Add vegetables and shrimp to batter and mix. (Use any combination of vegetables to make 1 cup.)
4. Drop by teaspoon into heated oil and deep fry.

– Contributed by Ritsuko Nishida.

SOBA (Japanese) Buckwheat noodles, sold fresh and dried. Traditionally eaten on New Year's.

SOMEN Japanese wheat-flour noodles which are like miniature spaghetti (vermicelli).

SOMEN SALAD See SALAD, SOMEN.

SOURSAP Big, yellowish-green fruit with prickly skin. Very juicy and fibrous pulp with tangy taste. Relative of breadfruit. Also called JACKFRUIT.

SOY SAUCE See SHOYU.

SOYBEAN Popular local snack. Soybeans are boiled in

salted water so that the skin becomes soft and it's easy to extract the soybean, either with teeth or fingers. Also the source of tofu (bean curd), and Chinese black beans. See also KINAKO.

SPAGHETTI WITH RICE Delicious local dish invented when the first local Japanese married an Italian.

SPAM A meat substitute which for some reason is about 10 times as popular in Hawaii as anywhere else in the U.S.

SPAM, HOW TO CAMOUFLAGE You can cook it shoyu sato style, fry it in an egg batter, mash it up and cook like hamburger patties, put in casseroles, or mash it in with your rice. You can even make SPAM MUSUBI.

SPAM MUSUBI Slice spam, fry it, and place on top of a rectangular (spam-shaped) musubi. Wrap a piece of nori around it.

SPARERIBS, BARBECUE PORK, RECIPE See PORK.

SPOON MEAT Soft flesh of a young coconut. Also used by older generation to refer to young unspoiled girls.

SPRING ROLL Oriental dish consisting of vegetables and pork or seafood wrapped in rice paper and deep fried.

SQUASH A plant of the gourd family, eaten as a vegetable. See also SEQUA, BITTER MELON, FUQUA, HUQUA, AND WINTER MELON.

SQUID Ocean mollusk. Often eaten dried, like cuttlefish or octopus. Also fried or in squid luau. Also called CALAMARI or IKA.

SQUID LUAU Local dish made with coconut, coconut milk, salt water, taro leaves and squid. When made with chicken it's called CHICKEN LUAU. See also LUAU, PALUSAMI.

SQUIRRELFISH Menpachi.

STAR ANISE Small, dried licorice-flavored spice used in Chinese cooking. See FIVE SPICE POWDER.

STARCH What locals eat a lot of.

STAR FRUIT Star-shaped fruit with thin, waxy, yellow-green rind. Also called carambola.

STEAMED MANAPUA, RECIPE See MANAPUA.

STINKFISH Another name for dried cuttlefish. See CUTTLEFISH.

STUFFED CABBAGE ROLLS, RECIPE See CABBAGE.

STUFFED EGGPLANT, BAKED, RECIPE See EGGPLANT.

SUGAR CANE Local snack you get by cutting a stalk of sugar cane, washing it, then chewing and sucking on the stalk.

SUKIYAKI (Japanese) Meat and vegetables cooked in shoyu-based sauce. The word originally comes from the Japanese for 'cooked on a spade.' Japanese farmers used to grill their meat out in the fields by using a spade or a hoe and holding it over the fire.

SALT SALMON SUSHI

1½ cup RICE
2 slices SALT
  SALMON
2 tsp. GINGER, sliced
  into thin shoestrings

1 tsp. BLACK SESAME
  SEED
4 tbsp. VINEGAR
½ tsp. SALT

1. Remove the skin and bones. Slice the salmon into thin pieces.
2. Combine the ginger, vinegar and sugar and mix. Soak the salmon in this sauce overnight. This will remove the salt and soften the salmon.
3. Cook the rice.
4. Remove salmon from the sauce and add the salt.
5. Combine the sauce and rice.
6. Add the salmon and mix.
7. You may either press the mixture through a sushi mold or make rice balls.
8. Sprinkle with black sesame seeds and serve.

– Contributed by Glenna Sakata.

SURGEONFISH Manini.

SUSHI Rice seasoned with vinegar sauce. See also SUSHI, VARIETIES.

SUSHI, VARIETIES Cone (Inari), Maki (Norimaki), Nigiri, Chirashi, Fukusa, and California Roll.

SWAMP CABBAGE Ong choi.

SWEET BREAD Pao doce.

SWEET BREAD USES French toast, fundraisers.

SWIPE Hawaiian moonshine. Often made from pineapple.

TAEGU (Korean) Shredded codfish or cuttlefish in a spicy sauce.

TAKENOKO (Japanese) Bamboo shoot.

TAKO (Japanese) Octopus.

TAKUWAN Japanese pickled daikon or turnip.

TAMAGO (Japanese) Cooked egg. See also FUKUSA.

TANGLAD (Filipino) Lemon grass. In Filipino cooking, used to season chicken or pork stews, or knotted and

---

CRISPY TAKUWAN

3 DAIKON, sliced
1¼ cup SUGAR
½ cup WHITE VINEGAR
¼ cup SALT

1 tsp. AJINOMOTO
Drops of YELLOW FOOD COLORING
½ CHILI PEPPER, chopped

Combine all of the above and leave in refrigerator for a couple of days, then serve.

– Contributed by Glenna Sakata.

placed in cavity of chicken before roasting to flavor. See also CITRONELLA, LEMON GRASS.

TARO A starchy root used to make poi and kulolo. The leaves are used as wrapping for steaming foods. Hawaiian staple.

TARO LEAVES Similar to spinach leaves. Also called luau leaves. See LUAU.

TEMPURA (Japanese) Lightly battered, deep-fried seafood or vegetables.

TEPPAN YAKI (Japanese) Meat and/or seafood, grilled with vegetables.

TERIYAKI (Japanese) Poultry or meat is first marinated in shoyu flavored with ginger, garlic and brown sugar, then grilled. Korean version is called BULGOGI.

PUPU STYLE TERI BURGER

1 lb. HAMBURGER
GREEN ONIONS,
 chopped
1 EGG
½ cup FLOUR (for rolling)

2 slices BREAD, mashed
 with water
SALT and PEPPER,
 to taste
OIL for frying

MARINADE:
2 cloves GARLIC,
 chopped up fine
2 tbsp. SHOYU

1 tbsp. SUGAR
1 tsp. MIRIN or SAKE

1. Mix marinade and leave in refrigerator overnight.
2. The next day, mix hamburger, bread, green onions, egg together.
3. Pour marinade into hamburger mixture and mix.
4. Make pupu-size (smaller than regular size) patties.
5. Put flour into any kine dish. Roll patties in flour.
6. Pan fry until brown.

– Contributed by Barbara Tong

TERMITES A little-known source of fats and protein. Can be eaten raw by grasping it by the wings, then

KOREAN TERIYAKI SAUCE

½ cup SHOYU
2 tbsp. SUGAR
½ tsp. SALT
½ tsp. BLACK PEPPER

4 tsp. SESAME SEEDS
  roasted and crushed
3 GREEN ONIONS,
  chopped
1 small clove GARLIC,
  crushed

Combine all ingredients and pour over one pound beef or chicken to be cooked. Marinate several hours in refrigerator before cooking.

– Contributed by Kathy Liu.

dashing it into your mouth and biting the little sucker before it can bite you.

THOUSAND YEAR EGGS (Chinese) Duck eggs coated with lime, clay, salt and ashes, and aged a few months.

TI LEAVES Shiny, oblong leaves of the ti plant, used to ornament or wrap foods for cooking.

TUNA, VARIETIES Albacore/Ahipalaha, Ahi/Yellowfin, Aku/Skipjack Bonito.

TUPIG Filipino dessert made out of mochiko and coconut milk, wrapped in banana leaves.

TILAPIA Local fish with a bad reputation and a bad smell. Lives in dirty water and eats stuff that we won't talk about here. We hear there's lots of research being done and money being spent to popularize tilapia as a food. Good luck.

TILAPIA, HOW TO TAKE AWAY SMELL Freeze 'em.

TOASTED COCONUT CHIPS, RECIPE See COCONUT.

TOFU Custardlike blocks of pressed pureed soybeans, usually packed in water. Also called BEAN CURD. See also KINAKO.

TOFU SALAD Salad made of alternating layers of tofu, watercress, tuna, onions (both green and round), tomatoes, and so on. Sauce optional.

TONKATSU Pork katsu. See KATSU.

TREE FERN Young shoots can be boiled until tender, then sliced and eaten. Also called KAGUMA, HAPUU.

TRIPE STEW Stew made from stomach lining of pigs. Popular local delicacy.

TSUBU See KUPIPI.

TSUKEMONO (Japanese) Pickled vegetables. Also called KOKO.

TUNA, VARIETIES Albacore/Ahipalaha, Ahi/Yellowfin, Aku/Skipjack/Bonito.

TUPIG Filipino dessert made out of mochiko and coconut milk, wrapped in banana leaves.

UALA Hawaiian word for sweet potato.

UDON (Japanese) Thick wheat noodles.

UHI Hawaiian for yam.

UHU (Hawaiian) Parrotfish.

UKU (Hawaiian) Grey snapper.

ULA ULA (Hawaiian) See ONAGA.

ULU Hawaiian word for breadfruit.

ULUA Fish, type of Jack, with firm white flakey flesh. Delicious panfried. Use the head for fish chowder. See also PAPIO.

UMANI (Japanese) Chicken and vegetables cooked in seasoned broth.

UME Known as Japanese plum, but it's a species of apricot. You often find an unripe ume in the middle of musubi. Soaked in brine and packed with red shiso leaves which makes it red and salty. Also called UME BOSHI. Sometimes made locally from Kokee plums.

UMU Samoan for IMU.

UNCLE BEN'S Haole rice (fluffy kine). See RICE, STYLES OF PREPARATION.

UNI (Japanese) Sea urchin. See WANA.

U'U (Hawaiian) See MENPACHI.

VANA See WANA.

VIENNA SAUSAGE Popular bento item, usually prepared Shoyu Sato style.

VINHA D'ALHOS (Portuguese) Commonly referred to as "Portuguese Roast". Meat marinated in a wine vinegar and garlic mixture (including chili pepper and rock salt) before cooking. Fish can be used instead of meat. Full name: CARNE DE VINHA D'ALHOS.

W

WAFFLE DOG Hot dog encased in batter and cooked. Sort of a hot-dog tempura.

WAHOO Another name for ONO.

WANA (Hawaiian) (Pronounced VAH-nah) Sea urchin with long, pointed spines. Japanese call it UNI.

WARABI (Japanese) Mountain vegetable. Called Water Fern or Bracken Fern. See WATER FERN.

WASABI (Japanese) Hot green horseradish. Comes in powder form which you mix with water to eat. Be careful! Hot stuff! Also called WASABE.

WATER CHESTNUTS Crispy, white walnut-sized vegetables with tough, brown skins and crisp, white meat. Can store fresh ones refrigerated for several days. After opening canned water chestnuts, you can drain and refrigerate them in water in a covered jar for as long as a month, changing the water daily. Now you know everything you ever need to know about water chestnuts.

WATERCRESS Herb which grows in or around water. The stem and leaves are used in soups or salads or as garnish. There's a big watercress farm right in front of Pearlridge Shopping Center.

WATERCRESS SALAD, KOREAN, RECIPE See NAMUL.

WATER FERN Warabi.

WATER FERN, HOW TO PICK AND PREPARE

Grows by streams in the mountains. Can be used in a soup or steamed and eaten with mayonnaise and/or shoyu. Can also be boiled.

WON TON

1 lb. GROUND PORK
1 tsp. SUGAR
SALT and PEPPER to taste
2 stalks GREEN ONION, chopped
½ lb. CHINESE FISHCAKE

1 tbsp. SHOYU
6 WATER CHESTNUTS, minced
WON TON WRAPPERS
WATER to dampen wrappers
OIL for frying

1. Mix first seven ingredients.
2. Place generous spoonful of mixture onto middle of won ton wrapper.
3. Dampen edges with water and press edges together with fingers to form a triangle.
4. Gently pull the bottom corners of the triangle down below the base.
5. Slightly overlap the tips of the two corners and pinch them together.
6. Fry in hot oil until golden brown and crispy.
7. Drain on paper towels.
8. VARIATION: Won ton may be cooked in a chicken broth soup, garnished with green onions, Chinese or mustard cabbage.
9. Makes 3 dozen.

– Contributed by Ann Corum, author of ETHNIC FOODS OF HAWAI'I.

WEDDING Good opportunity to eat lots of local food. Unless both sides haole, of course.

WEKE Variety of goatfish. Baby weke are called o'ama. See also O'AMA.

WINTER MELON Large watermelon-shaped squash with firm white pulp. Usually sliced, then boiled or steamed; sometimes steamed whole and served with soup inside.

WOK Chinese frying pan for stir-frying.

WON BOK Celery cabbage. Also known as Chinese cabbage. (Used to make kim chee.)

WON TON (Chinese) A dumpling made with won ton pi and filled with ground pork. You can deep-fry it, steam it or put it in soup.

WON TON MIN Noodle soup with won ton inside.

WON TON PI Sheet of dough used to make won ton.

WON TON PI CHIPS You guessed it – chips made of won ton pi.

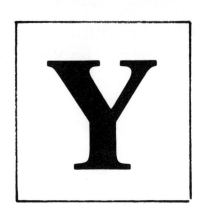

YAKIMONO (Japanese) Broiled or grilled foods.

YAKITORI Japanese shishkebab made with chicken.

YOKAN Japanese sweet made from gelatin and sweet azuki-bean paste.

YELLING AT TABLE, WHEN TO In Chinese restaurants. Careful or people will think you work there.

YES, WHEN TO SAY When a local person offers you food, it is very impolite to decline. So even if you hate the stuff, you eat some anyway, even if you have to spit it into the potted plants when they're not looking.

ZORIS (Japanese) Fishcake you wear on your feet. See KAMABOKO SLIPPERS.

BOOKS TO DA MAX

Let us know what you think about PUPUS TO DA MAX:

_____

_____

_____

_____

_____

_____

_____

_____

_____

Here are the prices*, if you'd like to order more copies of PUPUS and other PIDGIN TO DA MAX books:

ORDER BLANK

Please send me _____ copy(s) of **PIDGIN TO DA MAX**
@ $6.50 each. Total $_____ .
_____ copy(s) of **FAX TO DA MAX**
@ $7.50 each. Total $_____ .
_____ copy(s) of **PUPUS TO DA MAX**
@ $7.50 each. Total $_____ .

I'm enclosing my check or money order for $_____ , payable to BESS PRESS.

_____
Name (Please Print)

_____
Address

_____
City   State   Zip

*Prices include tax and handling charges. So no need add 'um! Allow 6-8 weeks for delivery.

BESS PRESS
P.O. Box 22388
Honolulu, HI 96822